THE GIRL ON THE TUBE

RACHEL ALLORD

Reformation
Lightning

Reformation Lightning

www.ReformationLightning.com

Designed and typeset by Pete Barnsley (CreativeHoot.com)

Printed in the UK

ISBN 978-1-916669-10-9

Reformation Lightning, an imprint of 10Publishing
Unit C, Tomlinson Road, Leyland, PR25 2DY, England

Email: info@10ofthose.com
Website: www.10ofthose.com

1 3 5 7 10 8 6 4 2

1

Grey pleated skirt.

Navy blazer.

Crisp white shirt.

Green stripped necktie. A *tie!*

I cannot *believe* I have to wear this getup. Every. Single. Day. This country is weird.

If it wasn't for the frizzy brown hair, I'd hardly recognize the girl in the mirror. I grab my brush and tug through my untamable mop.

"You ready?" Dad hollers from the kitchen.

"Almost!"

I give up. There's no fixing it. I find a hairband and twist and pull until my hair submits into a ponytail, then I slip my feet into my brand-new Mary Janes that Dad bought me earlier this week. Here in England, you can't wear any old shoes to school like you can in America, here you have to wear school approved shoes. Why this style of shiny black shoe with a strap jutting across the middle got the name *Mary Janes* I'll never know, but I decide my right shoe will be *Mary* and my left shoe will be *Jane*.

I examine myself in the mirror one last time from every angle. Front, back, and side. At least my room came with a full-length mirror attached to the wall.

My room.

But it's not really. *My* room is back home, in Wisconsin.

"Addie! You don't want to be late on the first day of school!"

"Coming Dad!" I grab my backpack and find Dad making toast in the kitchen.

"Look at you," he says. "Very smart."

"Why do I have to wear this?"

"Because all the kids in London wear school uniforms."

I sigh and ransack the fridge for the strawberry jam.

"Just think of the time you'll save by not having to decide what to wear every morning. Oh, I forgot." Dad thuds a small stout jar on the counter. "Someone at work gave me this to try."

"What's that?"

"*Marmite*. You eat it on toast I think."

I unscrew the yellow lid and dip my pinky into what looks like chocolate syrup, then pop my finger into my mouth. *Gag*! What is this, beef paste? Whatever it is, it's definitely *not* chocolate syrup! I gesture for Dad to quick get me a glass of water.

Dad grins. "I've heard it's an acquired taste." He hands me a cup and I swish water around my mouth to wash away the salty poison.

The toast pops. Dad spreads on a thick layer of strawberry jam and hands it to me. By the time I gobble it down, the butterflies in my gut have migrated to my throat, but I don't mention them. Dad wants me to be brave. So I take one last sip of orange juice, sling my school bag over my shoulder as Dad grabs his work bag, and we fly out the door.

Our apartment is on the fourth floor of a brick building south of the River Thames, not far from the high street that holds all the shops and restaurants. For the past month it's just been me and Dad and all of London. We munched fish and chips under the London Eye, and cruised past Big Ben, and even celebrated my twelfth birthday on September 1st by zipping up the elevator to the top of the pointy Shard building. But now, ready or not, it's time for school; for Dad to teach at the university and for me to start year seven.

We pass the Vietnamese restaurant that serves soft-as-pillow dumplings and merge into the current of people flowing toward the station.

"You remember how to get there?" Dad asks.

"First we take the green line."

"Right. The District line," Dad clarifies.

"Then we change to the blue line…"

"Piccadilly."

"And get off at… Barry's Court?"

"Close," Dad says. "*Barons* Court."

Up ahead, I spy the bright red circle with a horizontal blue bar through the middle that marks all of London's Underground stations. We hurry past the coffee kiosk and the purple flower hut and enter East Putney Station.

I dig out my travel card from my pocket and hold it against the electronic reader until the tiny light on the barricade flashes green. The barriers flap open, we step through, and Dad and I join a herd of strangers plodding up the stairs to the platform.

"Welcome to rush hour," Dad says.

Moments later, a train roars up. Everyone piles on. There aren't any seats left so I clutch the bright yellow safety handles dangling from the ceiling and execute a half pull up, my feet swinging off the ground. The train jerks forward. I lose my balance and drop down on a foot.

"Sorry," I say to the foot whose owner is wearing orange stripy socks and a serious grey suit.

He wordlessly scolds me with his eyes.

The train is brimming with kids in uniforms. A group of boys in maroon blazers and black ties huddles by the door. A cluster of students in grey blazers and red ties leans over a phone. Some of the kids are wearing navy blazers and dark green ties, just like me, which means we're heading to the same school.

Even though we're technically on the Underground, this part of the District line slithers up and over the sludgy brown Thames before dipping underneath the city. Up through the rooftops we sail, where the brick homes resemble white frosted gingerbread houses and the chimneys remind me of *Mary Poppins*.

At each station the train jolts to a stop, but not for long. The doors swish open, and everyone in the train squeezes toward the middle to make space for more people. Three girls in navy blazers get on, chatting as if they've known each other forever. They probably have. Just like my best friend Lauren and I have known each other since we were four. Lauren and I have always started school together. Except for today.

A hot lump claws my throat. One of the navy-blazer girls catches me staring at her. I quickly look above her head, to the advert sign of a yawning woman who needs vitamins.

"This is us," Dad says as we pull up to Earl's Court Station. The carriage doors open, and we tumble out. "Now what Addie girl?"

He's testing me. We practiced my school route a couple of days ago and he wants to see if I remember. The navy-blazer girls are heading towards the escalators, so I follow. "Down to the… the… pickle something line."

"Piccadilly."

We step on the escalator that transports us to the belly of the city. The biggest rule about riding escalators in London is to *stand on the right*. That way anyone late for work can blow past you on the left and not get any more annoyed than they already are. Down we descend, flashing past poster after poster of shows and concerts in the world above.

London is two cities really, one on top of the other. Above ground, it bustles with double decker busses and businesses and sights like Buckingham Palace. But underneath all of that you'll discover a whole other world, a labyrinth of tunnels where people scurry like mice and trains rush through giant tubes. The Underground holds London together. It keeps the city connected and flowing, like veins in a body.

The long escalator spits us out and Dad and I find the westbound platform and wait for the next train. I keep my toes behind the bright yellow line that reads *MIND THE GAP* and peer down the gloomy hole in the wall. Moments later, bright headlights pierce the dark tunnel. A train snakes up. The doors beep open and Dad and I clamber on.

The Piccadilly line is hot and smelly, much tighter and scummier than the wide airconditioned District line. Sweat trickles down my side. If only I could peel off this blazer! But we're jammed packed in this canister like socks stuffed in a drawer and I can't even lift my hands.

Another London rule: don't look anyone in the eye, especially on a crowded train. The more surrounded you are, the more you pretend other people don't exist, even if your nose happens to be trapped in someone's armpit. Passengers stare blankly into space or look at shoes, books, or phones, anything but one another. Unless, of course, you're riding with your Dad.

Dad catches my eye. *One stop*, he mouths as the rub of wheels against the rails heightens to a deafening screech.

Finally, we reach Barons Court. I push past passengers, hurdle over suitcases bound for Heathrow airport, and squeeze out the door.

Air. Space. Relief!

"We made it," Dad says unbuttoning his suit coat.

"I miss you driving me to school."

"You miss my singing, don't you?"

"Dad, your singing is the worst!"

If I were starting school back home in America, Dad could get me to school in six minutes flat. We'd jump in the car, zip to school, and he'd sing along to whatever happened to be playing on the radio, even if he didn't know the words. It's true, Dad is a terrible singer. But he's right, I miss it. And our car. And my old school. And having Lauren beside me.

We head up the steps, exit the station, and turn left.

"Dad?"

"Yeah."

"Lots of the kids ride the Tube on their own."

"No yellow school busses here."

"Some of them seemed to be my age."

"I suppose so."

We wait for the green man signal and cross the busy street. The school looms before me, proud and impressive looking in its sturdy brick exterior. My stomach twists and turns.

"Remember," Dad says, "this is the first day of high school for everyone in your year."

"But a lot of them will already know each other." My voice sounds weak, like someone is squeezing my throat.

"Some will, some won't. You'll do great. You're my brave girl. Don't be nervous."

How do you make yourself not be nervous? Is there a trick I should know?

Year seven is the bottom rung of high school and most of the students look older than me. Maybe the school forces everyone to dress the same so everyone feels as if they belong. It's not working. I don't belong. I may look like I fit in but deep down, I know the truth. I should be home.

What's more, Dad *really* doesn't belong at this school either. Where are the other parents? Nowhere. We're nearing the front entrance and I want to turn around. Head back to Wisconsin where I belong, where I should be starting sixth grade in new jeans and a carefully chosen t-shirt, surrounded by other kids – kids I've known since kindergarten, wearing new jeans and carefully chosen t-shirts.

London was cool for a while. Playing tourist with Dad was fun, but summer is over. We've hit real life. I'm ready to go home.

I spot the same trio of girls from the station. They look like they're having the time of their lives. One glances my way but not for long. Why should I matter to her? She's got friends and I'm just the new kid.

The first day of school used to be about swapping stories. Seeing friends you haven't seen all summer. Checking out everyone's outfits.

Not anymore. Now it's about keeping it together. Feeling like you're invisible *and* sticking out. Hoping to go unnoticed and wishing someone would see you. Survival.

"You ready?" Dad asks.

No. Not at all. My stomach hurts. For some reason I want to find a rock, a big, hard rock and throw it at the circle of chatty girls. Break them apart like bowling pins.

But I don't say any of these things to Dad. Instead, I force a smile.

"Ready."

2

"How'd it go?" Dad asks after school. He's waiting for me outside a coffee shop not far from the station.

"Alright."

"How was lunch?"

I shrug.

"Who did you sit with?"

"People." The cafeteria was crowded, I was surrounded by people. But sitting at a table where nobody talks to you is no better than eating alone.

"Did you get to know anyone?"

"I guess."

"Oh yeah? Like who?"

"I don't know! I don't know anyone, and nobody knows me!" I stomp toward the station.

Like I said, survival.

Back at the apartment, Dad leaves me alone until the doorbell rings. I run out of my room to see who it is. A package from Aunt Becky!

"Wonder what my sister sent us?" Dad says, slicing through the packing tape.

The box is bursting with all sorts of goodies, mostly stuff you can't find in London: packets to make ranch dip, the right kind of corn chips, and my all-time favorite, four boxes of macaroni and cheese. Dad tears open a bag of cheese balls straight away and tosses one toward my open mouth.

Dad then pops one into his own mouth. "The taste of home."

At the bottom of the box, I find a big square envelope with my name written on it in purple cursive. I take the card to my room and open it.

Dearest Addie,

Hey girl, I miss you! Enjoy the treats – but not all at once or else you'll have a stomachache! Take care of your dad and let him take care of you. Keep shining, keep dancing, and I'll keep praying for you.

Every bit of my love,

Aunt Becky

I reach under my bed and pull out my box that holds some of my precious things. A scrapbook that Lauren made for me. A goodbye card signed by everybody in my fifth-grade class. Tic-tac, the soft, orange kitten I've had since I was a baby. A book filled with pictures of me and my mom. I study my favorite, the two of us in our backyard, laughing and holding up bright red leaves from our maple tree. I flip through a few more pages then return to rummaging through the box. Shoved at the very bottom are my tap shoes.

Keep dancing, Aunt Becky told me.

Okay, Aunt Becky. You got it.

I wriggle into my tap shoes and tighten the laces, then head to the kitchen. Will I remember the choreography from last spring's dance recital? Just thinking about the routine, the lyrics begin to play in my head. I sure don't feel happy now, but I wonder if hearing the words "I'm happy" over and over might make it true. I ask Dad to cue up the music. He blasts it from the speaker, and I start pounding away on the kitchen floor for an invisible and adoring audience.

When the song ends, Dad claps and I take a bow.

Dad holds up the bag of Tootsie Rolls Aunt Becky sent. "Do you want to take these to school tomorrow? Maybe kids would like to try them."

Maybe. Maybe handing out candy makes people talk to you. Like tap dancing makes you feel better, at least while the music is playing. The noise drowns out the loneliness and your feet stomp out the sadness but then bam – just like that the song ends. The music fades and so does your happiness and you're back to feeling whatever you were feeling before.

"Can I FaceTime Lauren?" I ask as I pour myself some juice.

"It's still morning there."

Stupid time difference. "Can I stay up until she gets home from school?"

Dad looks doubtful.

"Please?"

He's caving, I can see it.

"I haven't talked to her in *forever*!"

He nods finally.

Hours later, Dad makes me get ready for bed before calling Lauren. With all of my teeth brushed and a few of them flossed, he sets up the laptop and hands it to me. Lauren giggles when she sees me all bundled up in bed.

"It's nighttime there? That's so weird!"

She tells me about her first day of school and I tell her about mine. "And sometimes you have to push through people just to get on and off the Tube," I explain. "You'll see when you come to visit."

"Okay."

"I can't wait!"

"Yeah, me too!"

After we hang up, I grab the flowery planner that Aunt Becky gave me last Christmas and flip to the last week in October where I printed *Lauren in London!* in big fat letters. Lauren has a few days off of school that week, so her mom said it might be a good time to try to visit.

I find my colored pens and doodle hearts and dots around the letters. Then I count backwards in the calendar until I hit today. Eight weeks. Lauren will be here in about eight weeks! If I didn't have this visit to look forward to, I just might squish myself into Aunt Becky's box and ship myself home.

Second day of school.

Wash face. Get dressed. Attempt to tame hair.

Give up. Eat breakfast. Brush teeth.

I stuff the Tootsie Rolls into my bag before Dad and I race out the door, then rush to the station, tap in, scramble to the platform, hop on the train seconds before the door closes, and hold on tight. The day has just started and I'm tired already.

The train slowly pulls away from the platform and I stare out the window, at the grumpy people left standing on the platform. I scan their drab clothes – the commuter uniform. Brown, grey, black. Dull, dull, dull.

And then... *pop!* A green hat in the crowd. Lush and happy, like the ferns that line the white siding of my old house. But it's not just that I've noticed the lady wearing it, she's noticed me. In fact, the lady in the green hat is staring straight at me. Her hair is dark, her lips are red, and her penetrating eyes follow mine. As the train moves past, her head turns with it, our gaze locks. Does she know me? Do I know her?

I crane my neck to see her as long as I can. We watch each other, uninterrupted, until the train ducks into a tunnel and we're cut off from each other's sight.

At lunch I sprinkle Tootsie Rolls on the cafeteria table. Ellie, a freckled redhead, snatches one. "What are these?"

"Tootsie Rolls," I say. "From America. Try one."

She untwists the wrapper and sniffs the sweet before popping it into her mouth. "Mmm. Gorgeous!"

The girl beside her, Victoria, takes one too. "I've had these before."

"Have you?" Ellie asks. "When?"

"When I visited my aunt in Chicago. Everything in America is excessively sugary."

"That sounds brilliant!" Ellie says. "I love sugar."

At the end of our table, close enough to join us if she wants to, sits a girl with long, black hair. I recognize her from my English class. I glance her way, hoping she knows she can help herself.

"I've not been to Chicago," Ellie says, unwrapping another, "but I have been to Florida."

All of a sudden, I notice something, something important. Ellie isn't wearing a skirt. "Hey! I didn't know we could wear pants!" I blurt out.

Victoria and Ellie erupt with laughter.

"I should hope we're all wearing pants!" Ellie manages. "Especially to school!"

I look down at my skirt, confused.

More giggles. "Victoria, tell her!" Ellie says. "She doesn't know!"

Victoria looks at me like I'm an idiot. "You mean to say *trousers*. And yes, skirts aren't compulsory. Trousers are acceptable if they're part of the school uniform." She says each word crisply, like she's practicing to be a news reporter on the BBC.

I shrug. "Trousers. Pants. Same thing."

"No, it's *not* the same thing. Not at all. Pants are," she lowers her voice, "*knickers*."

"Underwear," Ellie clarifies.

My face grows hot. "Oh. Weird. Hey, have you guys ever tried Jolly Ranchers? I'll bring some tomorrow."

Ellie's eyes light up. "Brilliant!"

Victoria seems to be studying me. "You were on my train this morning, weren't you?"

"I don't know, maybe."

"You were. I saw you. Was that your dad next to you?"

I nod.

Victoria's eyebrows lift in surprise. "Did he actually travel all the way to school with you? Does he do that *every* day?"

I take a big bite of my sandwich. It's not so much *what* Victoria is saying that rubs me wrong, it's *how* she's saying it.

"Must be such a bother for him to travel all that way, just to make sure you and your sweets arrive at school safely. But I suppose, if that's what he must do." She shrugs her shoulders and pops a piece of candy, *my* candy, that Aunt Becky sent all the way from America, into her mouth. Then she crumples the wrapper in her fist.

I turn my attention to the quiet girl at the end of the table. Finally, she glances up. I slide her a Tootsie Roll and she looks surprised. Slowly and carefully she unwraps it.

After school, I tell Dad he doesn't need to travel with me. None of the other parents do. He's putting away the groceries we picked up on the walk home and I'm bouncing a tennis ball I found outside our building on the kitchen floor.

"I can get to school on my own, Dad. I really can."

"You're not ready, Addie."

"That way you can get to work when you want to."

"The department knows I need to be flexible, at least for the first few months."

"But I don't *need* you to come with me!" How do I make him understand?

"Addie, it's not open for discussion."

"But all the kids travel to school on their own."

"All the kids who have grown up in London maybe. You're not used to how things work here yet. You only just moved here."

"Yeah, well *whose fault is that?*" I slam the ball hard against the floor. It lands on the counter and knocks over the yogurt. "You're the one who wanted to move here," I shout. "You're the one who told me to be brave!"

Dad goes still. He looks at me sternly. "Addie, pick up the yogurt."

I clench my teeth, not looking away. And I *don't* touch the yogurt. Instead, I grab the tennis ball and storm out the front door. In the hallway, I climb halfway down the flight of stairs and sit. A moment later, from above me, I hear our apartment door open and quietly shut. Dad's checking up on me.

I throw the tennis ball at the opposite wall. It bounces off and comes back, but I fail to catch it. I retrieve the ball, sit down, and try again. After a few attempts I find the rhythm and catch it several times in a row. Smack against the wall, bounce on the floor, thump into my hand. Wall, floor, hand. Wall, floor, hand. Over and over.

Suddenly, the door to 2A opens. The ball zooms past a woman's face. She gasps, steps backwards. I shoot to my feet. The ball dribbles against the floor.

The woman gapes at me. "Does this look like a tennis court? Have I stepped into Wimbledon?"

"Sorry." The ball pitters to a stop.

"This is a corridor of residency," the lady continues. "People *live* beyond these walls. These doors lead to people's homes."

I collect the ball and stand there, head down. She's not finished being angry with me I don't think.

She takes a step closer. We're about the same height but she's old, like my grandma, with short, silver hair. "I've not seen you before. Is this building your home?"

"No," I mumble. *Home* is Wisconsin. *Home* is a house surrounded by fresh smelling pine trees and a room with a window that overlooks a rambling backyard.

"You don't live in this building?"

"I mean, yes. I live here."

She looks at me impatiently. "Make up your mind, child. Yes or no?"

"I live here now. But I haven't for long. Me and my dad moved in a month ago."

"My *dad* and *I*."

"Huh? Oh. *My dad and I* moved here a month ago. From America."

The woman sighs. "Indeed."

I better smooth this over. The last thing I want is a cranky old woman telling on me. I whip up my best smile and thrust out my hand. "I'm Addie. Addie Brown. Nice to meet you."

The woman stares at me as if I've turned blue. "Well Addie Brown, I suppose I should reply *it's lovely to meet you too* but given the present circumstances, that wouldn't be entirely true. Tell me, why are you in the corridor abusing the wall?"

I shrug. "I don't know. I was bored."

"You ought to take the game outside."

"It's raining."

She glances beyond me to the narrow window. "So it is. You live upstairs? I reckon it's your footsteps I hear at night, you and a brother or sister I presume."

"No. Just me and my dad. I mean, my *dad* and *I*."

"No, you were right the first time. No brothers or sisters? Then tell me Addie Brown, how is it that you produce such a racket on your own?"

"Oh, that might be the tap dancing."

"*Tap* dancing."

"I'm a tap dancer. I took lessons back home."

"And now you've tap-danced your way across the pond."

"Well I don't take lessons here in London yet, but I brought my tap shoes and sometimes I practice on the kitchen floor."

"Aren't I the fortunate one? Have you ever considered that *your* floor happens to be *my* ceiling? You should reflect on that the next time you impersonate Ginger Rogers."

"Ginger *who*?"

"Ginger Rogers. You've not heard of Ginger Rogers? She was a dancer years ago. An *American* like you but she danced on stage and on the big screen instead of other people's ceilings."

"If I had a stage I'd tap on that too, but I don't so I have to use the only floor I've got. I can't help where I live. It's not my fault my floor happens to be your ceiling."

She gasps. "Aren't you a cheeky one?"

"I am really sorry about the noise. I wasn't trying to bother you and you're right, I didn't think about who might be living underneath me. But when *would* it work?"

She continues to study me.

"For me to tap dance I mean. When could I tap dance in my kitchen and not bother you?" I give the ball a single thump on the floor, catch it in my hand, and wait for her reply.

The silver-haired lady is silent for so long I don't think she'll ever answer. "Thursday afternoons," she finally says. "I visit my son then. Saturdays are fair game as well."

"Okay. It's a deal."

I'm about to offer my hand again, so we can shake on it, but just then I notice a glint of color against her grey sweater. I step closer to examine the tiny pendant hanging from her necklace. "A peacock! I've never seen a peacock on a necklace before. But I have seen one in real life, with its feathers all fanned out, have you? My dad and I waited at the zoo for hours to see it."

"It is a rather breathtaking sight, isn't it?" she says, fingering the small turquoise bird.

I want to reach out and touch the dainty charm, but I hold back. "Well, see you later. Sorry about the noise. I'll try to be quieter."

I'm halfway up the flight of stairs when I hear, "Would you like to come for tea?"

I stop. Turn around. Clomp down a few steps. "Me?"

"Your bouts of boredom may drive you to unwind the firehose next and we wouldn't want that, would we? Next Tuesday," she says. "After school. If your father allows it."

Is she serious? After I nearly take off her nose with a tennis ball, she invites me to tea? Why would she want to have tea with me? I don't want any tea, especially with her, but I'm stuck. I owe her. "Sure. I guess so."

She frowns at my response.

"I mean, thank you."

"Lilian," she finally tells me. "I'll aim to meet your father in the next few days. Until then, Addie Brown." Then she turns and disappears into her apartment.

I bounce the ball one more time on the floor, then gallop up the stairs.

That night, I FaceTime Lauren. I tell her about Lilian and the tennis ball and the weird invitation to tea.

Lauren tells me her locker is next to Jake Masters. She has second period with both Madison and Bethany and they're all working on a geography project together.

She and Madison are going roller skating next week.

The whole sixth grade class is heading to Green Bay for a field trip.

There's a high school football game on Friday and everyone will be there.

After we hang up, I don't brush my teeth. Instead, I hang over the side of my bed, pull out the box, release Tic-tac, and tuck his soft little body under my chin. It's a babyish, stupid habit but I'm glad he made the move with me. He's the same old ratty thing he's ever been, even if everything around me has changed.

Even Lauren.

3

I'm on the Tube, bending over to adjust the strap on Jane, when I notice another black pair of Mary Janes among the flock of feet. I look up. It's the girl from the end of the lunch table, the quiet one with long dark hair. She and a slightly older girl, her sister probably, are standing a few people away from me. As we zip along, I strain to eavesdrop on their conversation so I can catch her name. But the train roars loud and their voices stay quiet, so I never do.

Not until English class, a few hours later, when she answers correctly and Miss says, "Well done, Parisa." I grab my pencil. Taking a stab at the spelling, I scrawl her name on the inside of my notebook:

Pa – ris – a.

Toward the end of the lesson, Miss announces that we can work with a partner to finish up our simple/complex sentences worksheet. Students shuffle around and switch seats, but no one approaches me.

I take a breath. Heart thumping, I stand up and move toward Parisa's desk. "Wanna partner up?" I say all in a rush.

She seems surprised to see me, but then smiles. "Okay."

I slide into the empty desk behind her. Parisa turns around and reads the first simple sentence from the worksheet: "*Many people prefer vanilla ice cream.*" Her dark eyebrows knot in thought. "How should we convert this into a complex sentence?"

I think for a moment. "Many people prefer vanilla ice cream… because they've never tried cookies and cream!"

Parisa grins. "Or saffron ice cream."

"Saffron ice cream? Is saffron a type of candy?"

Her smile grows wider. "No, it's a spice."

"Never heard of it."

"It's my favourite."

"Where do you find saffron ice cream?"

"It's in some shops in London but everywhere in Iran."

We take a minute to write down our answers and then she asks, "Are you from America?"

"Yep."

"I thought so," Parisa says. "You sound like you should be on TV."

"I do?"

"Yes. Your accent."

"That's so weird. I didn't even know I had an accent until I moved here!"

"Neither did I!"

We continue going through the worksheet, chatting between each problem. Work and chat, work and chat until the bell rings and we gather our books and head for the door. Parisa waits for me by my locker and then I wait for her by hers and as we make our way to the cafeteria for lunch, we're still talking.

Parisa and I set our trays by Ellie and Victoria. Ellie greets us with a big "Hiya!" Victoria scoots over to make room. I open my milk and take in our foursome. I'd still rather be back at Washington Middle School, with Lauren and Madison and the rest of the gang, but at least I'm not alone. I'm one of four. Even if one of them includes know-it-all Victoria.

Later that evening my stomach growls like a wild beast. It's supper time, but I don't pick up on any sounds or smells coming from the kitchen yet. I'm lying on my back, dangling my head over the edge of my bed and studying my upside-down reflection in the mirror, my hair fanning out like the sun. I flip my legs over my head to stand and wander to the kitchen.

Dad's staring at his laptop screen on the table. His body is here, right in front of me, but the rest of him seems faraway. He does this often, stares into space. I call it his sad trance and it's my job to break it.

"Knock-knock," I say.

"Hm?"

"Knock-knock." I rap my knuckles on the table.

He blinks and gives me one of his fake, pinched smiles. "Who's there?"

I have no idea, I realize. I hadn't thought that far. I glance around the room and spot the salt and pepper holder. "Pepper."

"Pepper who?"

"Pepper... Peperoni pizza is on the menu tonight!"

"You think so, huh?" He smiles for real and pulls me close. "What would I do without my little comedian. Pepperoni pizza it is. Are we staying in or going out?"

"Out. Definitely out!"

Twenty minutes later we're making our way up the busy high street, past a homeless lady jangling a cup of coins and the gross but fascinating street sign covered in wads of chewed up gum. When we're about to cross, Dad extends his hand but I pretend not to notice. I'm in secondary school now. I don't want to hurt his feelings but aren't I too old? I tuck my hands into my pockets. Dad glances my way but doesn't say anything.

We stop in front of a restaurant with a bright red awning and a wooden sign that says *Aldo's.* "How about Italian food?"

The waiter asks Dad if we'd like the table by the window and Dad asks the waiter for a pepperoni pizza.

"*Sí, Sí.* Pepperoni, salami, pancetta..." The waiter says, pointing to a picture of a pizza on the menu topped with all sorts of meats.

"*Benissimo*," Dad says, showing off the little Italian he knows. "I think we're in store for some authentic Italian pizza," he says after the waiter leaves.

I was in the mood for your standard American pepperoni pizza, but I keep my mouth shut. This is not the time to complain. I've got a question to ask and I want the answer to be *yes*. If a pizza loaded with meat puts Dad in a good mood, we can get whatever pizza he wants.

Dad leans back in his chair, "So, you survived your first week of school."

Survived. Exactly.

"Do you like your teachers?"

"Some of them. My English teacher is nice, but things are strange here. Did you know that Math is called *Maths* and the letter Z is called *Zed* and sentences don't end with a period but a *full stop*? Oh, and guess what else? School goes on forever. We don't get out until the middle of July!"

"At least you get a break every six weeks."

The waiter appears and sets down our soft drinks. The bubbles tickle my nose as I slurp. "Dad, where's Iran?"

"Iran? It's by Iraq."

"Where's Iraq?"

"By Iran." Dad grins at his dumb joke. "In the Middle East. Here." He pulls up a map on his phone and shows me Iran nestled between Iraq and Afghanistan.

"There's a girl at school from Iran. She moved here last year."

"Oh yeah?"

"Yeah, her name's Parisa. She's really nice. And guess what? She's on the same train as me."

"That's cool."

I poke my straw around in my soda. "Yeah and her older sister is on our train, too."

"Nice." Dad says, still looking at his phone.

"So, I was thinking, since I know Parisa..."

Still scrolling.

"...and she has an older sister..."

No eye contact.

"...I could travel to school with them. Instead of you."

Dad looks up. "Addie we've been over this."

"I know people on the train now."

"Earl's Court is a confusing station."

"But I know exactly what to do and where to go. I've done it all week. It's easy."

"Addie, I've already told you *no*. You're not ready."

I cross my arms and shift my chair and turn away from him. He's so unfair! *He's* the one who decided to move us here. He's the one who proclaimed London "the coolest city in the world" with loads of opportunities. He's the one who pushed me to try new things. Well now that I want to try something new and get to school on my own, he won't let me.

The pizza arrives and I don't budge. Dad sets a slice on my plate. Deliciousness wafts up and fills my nostrils and ignites the hunger storm in my stomach but I don't move. I'm not going to take a bite. That'll show him!

"*Deliziosa*!" Dad says, reaching for a second slice.

After a minute I shift in my chair and rethink my strategy. Dad doesn't seem at all bothered and he just might polish off this pizza without me. Besides, I'm too hungry to think straight. I pick up my slice and bite off the chewy point of the triangle. This is not your standard American pepperoni pizza; this is better. Not that I'm going admit that to anyone or anything.

"Tell you what," Dad says wiping his hands on a napkin. "Let's have a trial. I'll travel with you, but I'll keep my distance. Pretend I'm not there and we'll see how it goes."

"But you will be there."

"Right, in case you get stuck or lost or need help."

I sigh.

"That's the deal kiddo. Take it or leave it."

I reach for another slice. "I'll take it."

4

Lilian's apartment is a cluttered museum. Framed art covers the walls, books pile in the corners, trinkets and vases and photographs pop up everywhere.

"How do you take your tea?" Lilian asks as she leads me past a couch covered in pillows of every size, shape, and color.

"Um… in a cup?"

"I'll sort it for you."

Her kitchen is just as jumbled. She drops a couple of teabags into a squat yellow teapot and flips on a kettle that plugs into the wall. Nothing like the tea kettle that sat on our stovetop back home, a metal thing that we only ever used to make hot chocolate on snow days. The water boils in no time. Lilian pours the hot water into the yellow teapot and then wraps a little quilt around it.

"What is that?" I ask.

"A tea cozy. It keeps the tea warm. Do sit down." She nods in the direction of the kitchen table.

I lower myself into a chair…

"Meoooooow!"

Yikes and wowzers, I've sat on a cat! A furious, hissing, yellow-eyed cat!

"I didn't see him!" I cry.

I should leave. Walk right out the door. First, I nearly take her out with a tennis ball and now I go and crush her cat.

But Lilian seems unbothered. She waves her hand in the air. "Oh, don't mind Earl Grey. He's a temperamental old creature." She scoops up the fat, grey cat and drops him to the floor. He saunters off a few paces but stops and turns around to glare at me. His face looks all smooshed in, but I don't think that's my fault. It's his breed. At least I hope so.

Lilian pours two cups of tea. She adds a heaping scoop of sugar and a splash of milk to one and hands it to me.

Be polite, I command myself. But the truth is, I can't stand tea. I only drink it when I'm ill, when Dad or Aunt Becky force it on me. I stir for as long as I possibly can and then manage a sip. Hopefully the drama classes I took last summer will pay off.

Lilian holds up a plate of cookies. "Biscuit?"

I slide one from the plate. "Why don't you call these cookies?"

"Because they're not cookies, they're biscuits."

"I've had biscuits before. This isn't a biscuit."

"Oh? Enlighten me then, what's a biscuit?"

"A bready, soft roll. You know, like biscuits and gravy. Or fried chicken and biscuits. My Aunt Becky makes the best chicken and biscuits when she comes to visit. In my old house I mean. Not here in London."

"I suppose it's been quite a move from your house in Wisconsin to a flat in London."

I bite off a corner of Lilian's dry and crumbly cookie. "Yeah, everything is different here," I explain, brushing crumbs from my school skirt. "The streets are noisier, and the houses are all squashed together, and I miss our big backyard."

"I'd imagine so."

"And another thing, back home, Dad drives me to school. Here I take the Tube, even though he doesn't let me ride it on my own."

"Fortunate girl," Lilian says.

"Fortunate?"

"To have a father who cares enough to accompany you to school until you learn the way. Some fathers don't bother knowing their children's whereabouts. A fortunate girl indeed."

"I guess so."

I help myself to another cookie. They're nothing special but they might help the tea go down. "Do you get any snow here?"

"Only occasionally."

"We get heaps of snow in Wisconsin. My best friend Lauren and I go sledding on the hill behind my house."

"We call that *sledging,*" Lillian says.

I plunk my cup on the table. "Why are words so different here?"

Lilian chuckles. "Silly child, it's you Americans who've dropped *U's* and mangled perfectly good pronunciations. *You* originated from *us*."

I sit back in my chair. I grip my cup and sip. Grip and sip. Last year in school we watched a video about the early Americans dumping barrels of tea into Boston harbor. It was their way of telling the English they'd *had it*. They were done with their rules and it was time *to break free*. How quickly can I dump this liquid down my throat and do the same?

We sit quietly for a while. "You're not wearing your peacock necklace today," I say to interrupt the silence.

"No. I don't wear it every day."

"Was it a present from someone?"

"It was in fact. From my husband. Nigel."

"Is he at work right now?"

Lilian looks at me in surprise. "Oh, no. Nigel has passed."

"Oh."

Outside, a siren whistles in the distance. Inside, here in this room with this lady I barely know, feels uncomfortably quiet. Lilian doesn't seem to mind. She seems fine with the pauses in our conversation. Every now and then she asks questions like where do I go to school, or what have I seen in London, or what do I like to eat. I answer and then go back to sipping in silence and watching the airplanes skim the rooftops outside her window.

"More tea?"

"No!" I say too quickly. I've only just managed to swallow most of it down, I'm not about to take more! "But thank you. I should probably get going so I can do my homework."

When Lilian ushers me back through the eclectic living room, my eyes land on a photograph of her standing next to a tall man in a tweed coat. Dead Nigel, probably. Next to them is a picture of a younger man with the same eyes and nose as Lilian. Her son maybe?

At the door Lilian says, "Until next week then."

My head snaps back to look at her. "Huh?"

"Next Tuesday I'll show you the proper way to eat a scone."

"Okay?" When did I agree to another Tuesday tea?

Earl Grey leaps to the arm of the sofa and gives me a death stare. Too bad, too. I like cats. We could have been friends. But I suppose I can't really blame him. I would be suspicious of someone four times my size who sat on me.

Lilian unlatches the door and I remember my manners. "Thank you for the tea and cook… and crunchy biscuits." And because it seems right, like it's a way to apologize for my blunders, I grasp the hem of my school skirt and curtsey.

Lilian presses her lips together. I can't help thinking she's trying not to smile. What have I done wrong now?

As promised, Dad keeps his distance as we travel to and from school. We don't stand together when we wait for the train on the platform. We don't sit by one another once we board. Sometimes we're not even in the same carriage.

This is what I wanted. To be separated from Dad. To do this by myself. So why do I feel lonelier than ever? Why does my throat feel tight and my stomach as shaky as this train?

From where I'm standing by the door, I glance over the sea of heads. Brown hair, blond hair, black hair… *pop!* Green. There it is again. The green hat, way on the other end of the carriage.

When the train stops at the next station, I decide to worm my way through passengers to try and get closer, but a pack of businesspeople shove on board and block my path. I'm stuck between a woman who sprayed herself with too much perfume and a man who's nodding his head to the music in his headphones. If I duck under his armpit, I can see the lady in the green hat.

From the neck down, her grey skirt and matching jacket blend in with the crowd, but her green hat sticks out like a tree in the desert. There's something about her that doesn't seem real, like she's stepped out from a movie. An old movie. The black and white kind my grandparents watch. She clasps a safety handle with one hand and an open book with the other. Her dark hair lands on top of her shoulders in a neat, soft curl. She lets go of the handle, turns a page of her book, and the corners of her mouth tip upwards.

What is she reading?

Where is she going?

How does she get her hair so glossy?

Twisting a lock of my frizz around my finger, I watch her, wishing she'd notice me. As the train slows for my stop, I push my way through to the door. The lady glances up and catches my eye. She recognizes me, I can tell.

Who is she? Out of everyone in the crowd, why does she seem to know me? I step off the train, sensing she's watching my every move.

"You're like a spy," I tell Dad as we walk home from school that afternoon.

"More like your guardian angel," he says.

"But I *haven't* needed you."

"You're right. You haven't."

"I'm not really alone, you know. I mean there are so many kids traveling to school on the train with me. Parisa and her sister are there somewhere. And the lady in the green hat."

He looks at me. "The lady in the *what*?"

"The lady in the green hat. She seems..." I stop. What? What does she seem like? Mysterious? Welcoming? Safe? "She seems like she'd help me if I needed it."

"This is someone you've met?"

"No. But we're on the Tube together. How could you have missed her, Dad? She's wearing a *green hat*!"

"Haven't noticed her. But I have noticed that you've done really well. In fact..."

I stop in my tracks.

He turns to face me. "I think you're ready to go on your own."

"*Yes!*"

"But Addie, listen. This is important. You are not allowed to travel anywhere except to and from school. Understood? Nowhere else."

I side hug him. "I promise."

That night I FaceTime Lauren and tell her.

"Oh okay," is all Lauren says. She's picking off the nail polish from her fingernails and doesn't even look up. She's always done it. As soon as the color dries, she starts chipping it off. "Guess what?" she says.

"What."

"Mrs Byrd moved our seats in English class today."

"So?" I say, studying the ends of my hair.

"So I'm not sitting next to Madison anymore. It's so unfair! We weren't talking *that* much."

We're both silent for a minute. I glance at my desk and spot my beautiful planner. Everything will be better when Lauren's here in person.

"Has your mom bought the tickets yet?"

Lauren looks at me blankly. "Tickets?"

"Plane tickets silly! For when you come in October."

"Oh that. Not yet."

"Well hurry up! I'll make a plan of stuff we can do."

"Okay. Hey, my mom's calling me. I've gotta go. My piano lesson's today and I've hardly practiced."

We say goodbye. I rummage in my desk drawer for my favorite pen with the aqua ink and grab my planner. Then I flop back down on my bed, find the last page in October, and make a list in the memo section.

What to show Lauren in London:

My apartment

My school

Parisa

Lilian and Earl Grey

Aldo's pizza

The Tube when it's really smelly and crowded

The sign on the high street with all the gum stuck over it

The homeless man with the dog

Big Ben

I recap the pen and use the top of it to count the days before Lauren's arrival. Thirty-two. Thirty-two days until I get to see my best friend for real. If she still is my best friend that is.

What am I talking about? Lauren and I are bonded solid. Before the move, we buried a bracelet in my backyard that proves it. *Best Friends Forever* the little charm reads. We bought it in one of those gumball-prize machines at Walmart and decided that instead of taking turns wearing it, we'd hide it. Our own buried treasure. Our secret that seals our loyalty.

Although she and Madison sure seem to be hanging out an awful lot. What if Lauren has found a new best friend?

No, I reassure myself, imagining our bracelet hidden in layers of dirt. But thinking about the trinket doesn't squelch the doubt that pesters like a mosquito. Even tucking Tic-tac under my chin fails to offer much comfort.

5

Monday, school.

Tuesday, school.

Wednesday, more school.

Thursday, guess what? School.

Now it's Friday, another day of tie-wearing, teacher-pleasing, rule-keeping, school.

That's what makes school so hard. The everyday-ness of it.

The day starts off with me cowering at my desk in French class. This is the first foreign language class I've ever taken, and it shows. I know a few Italian words, but this school doesn't offer Italian. So while the other kids can prattle off useful expressions like *où est la bibliothèque?* I can count to ten. That's about it.

Mademoiselle scans the classroom for a target, and I keep my eyes glued to the top of my desk, praying she won't call on me.

"Adeline?"

Rats! That's me! I meet her gaze.

"Comment allez-vous?"

My mind goes blank. She's asking, *how are you*? That much I know. What I don't know is how to answer. Think, Addie, think! How am I? How am I?

How do you say *nervous* in French?

How do you say, *confused beyond belief*?

The only word I can remember is the same word I always give, even though it's hardly ever true. "*Bien.*"

"*Ah, bien,*" Mademoiselle repeats, looking disappointed. She moves on to another student, a brighter student, a student who can actually hold a conversation and cause her to beam with teacherly pride.

Next up is gym, or "PE" as it's called here. We're playing football, which is the same thing as soccer. We change into our kits in the locker room before heading outside.

"Nice socks," someone says as we jog to the pitch.

I look down at my feet. Then I notice everyone else's feet. All the other students are wearing thick socks that go up to their knees. Everyone except me because Dad forgot to pick up football socks that I forgot to tell him I needed.

After changing out of my PE kit and back into my school uniform, I stumble into Math where the air swells with heat. All day the sky's been teasing rain but refuses to give in. Every hour feels more miserable than the last and I can't wait to go home and change into shorts and a tank top.

I take my seat behind Oliver Ridley. I don't know if there's such a thing as a professional sleep inducer but if there is, my Math teacher, Mr Stevenson, should switch careers. His voice is as interesting as the bare white walls of this room. No variety. No enthusiasm. No fun.

I prop my elbow on my desk and place my chin in my hand. One, two, three, four. Oliver Ridley has four moles on the back of his neck. His blond hair looks extra curly today, so I switch from mole counting to curl counting.

Sir drones on and on and the room grows hotter and hotter. I'm going to die of heat or boredom or both! The windows are open, but no breeze flutters in. If only I could free myself from this blazer! I tug my button-down shirt back and forth trying to get some air flow, but it hardly helps. Sir turns his back to us, still droning on about fractions. I shift in my seat until I'm hidden behind Oliver's mop. Then I skew my tie and undo my top button. Phew! A little better.

Minutes later, when we're working out problems on our own, Sir paces in between the rows like a jail warden. He stops at my desk. "Addie Brown?"

I look up. "Yes, Sir?"

He taps the knot of his tie and raises his eyebrows. "Top button."

"Oh, well, you see, I just came from PE," I explain. "I'll probably get more answers right if I'm not sweating like a pig."

A couple of students snicker.

Mr Stevenson's frown deepens. He leans closer. "Button. Up."

I sigh. You would think a teacher would appreciate my commitment to producing the best work possible, even in this heat, but you'd be wrong.

I button up.

Next is English. Miss Thompson stands by the door to greet us as we file in and, at the beginning of class, announces, "Given it's unbearably hot today, you may take off your blazers."

I want to run up and hug her.

English is my last class before lunch, before Parisa, Ellie, Victoria, and I make our way to the cafeteria together. While I'm eating lunch in London, my friends in America are just about to wake up. My school day is half over and theirs hasn't even started.

Soon Lauren and Madison and everyone in Wisconsin will be picking out what to wear, slurping down cereal, and sprinting through their big front yards to catch a yellow school bus. Or they'll scramble into cars and their moms will drop them off in front of school. Moms usually do drop off and pick up. That's what Lauren's mom does. That's what most moms do, I think.

I glance at the clock. Five more minutes to endure. Then I can shut off the thinking section of my brain, the part that has to interpret directions and discern accents and keep my body relatively still in my desk. Soon I can breathe a little. At lunch you can move and talk and not worry about making a mistake. Well, not a huge one anyway.

The second hand on the clock slices through the last few seconds of class. Five, four, three, two…

"Have a pleasant weekend," Miss Thompson says as we all bolt for the door.

"What did your dad say?" Parisa asks me once we're in the corridor. "Can you come over and stay for dinner?"

"Yep!"

Her smile brightens her whole face. "Oh, I'm glad. My mum is making *ghormeh sabzi.*"

I'm glad too, but her mom is making *what*? Is it safe to eat something you can't pronounce? I mean, I really like Parisa, but I've never been to her house before and I'm starting to worry about what they might put in front of me and expect me to stick in my mouth. What do people eat in Iran? A month ago, I couldn't even find it on a map so how am I supposed to know what their food is like? What if it's gross and I can't get it down?

"It's my favourite dish," Parisa says. "I can't wait for you to try it."

"Yeah, me too," I lie.

Parisa's favorite dish looks like sick. I'm not kidding. I don't want to be rude but as I view the strange looking food covering Parisa's table, my panic grows. I'd do just about anything for a nice comfortable bowl of macaroni and cheese. The only thing I recognize is the rice, and even that is topped with a suspicious looking oily brown drizzle. What am I going to do?

Parisa's Dad says a little prayer. I do too. *Please God help me to swallow and smile.*

After the *Amen*, Parisa's mom looks at me with kind eyes. "Please help yourself, Addie."

I take two scoops of rice and spread it around my plate. Maybe if my plate is covered in rice, nobody will notice if I don't take anything else. Nope. Parisa hands me the scariest dish of them all, a bowl of green slop with floating chunks. "What is this?" I ask.

"I told you! *Ghormeh sabzi*!"

"Yes... but... what *is* it?"

"Meat and vegetables and herbs," Parisa's mom explains. "If you don't like it, it is okay. You don't have to eat it."

"It's good," Jasmine promises. "You'll like it. Try it."

"Taste and see!" Parisa's dad echoes.

There's no escaping. They're all watching. No one is outright staring at me, but as Parisa's family pass dishes around and take bites, I know they're secretly waiting for my verdict. No matter how scared I am, I have to be brave. No matter how gross the food tastes, I have to be nice. *No gagging, Addie!* I command myself.

I scoop a tiny portion of the green slop onto my plate and move it around with my spoon.

After a minute, Parisa grins at me and nudges my elbow. *What are you waiting for?* her eyes say.

I dip the tip of my spoon into the green glop. Slip the spoon into my mouth. Courageously swallow. It's not awful.

I brave another spoonful, this time with more sauce and a bean. Not bad, really. This time I scoop a morsel of meat. Warm, tender, and rich, kind of like Dad's beef stew.

"It's good," I say. "Really good." I'm not lying, not one little bit.

Parisa's mom beams.

"Taste and see!" Parisa's dad repeats, raising his glass.

"Now try the *tahdig*." Parisa points to fragments of flat bread laying on top of the rice.

I take one. Crunchy and delicious. I try the bright, vegetable salad and the cucumber yogurt. Not amazing but they don't make me gag. None of it does. In fact, the *ghormeh sabzi* is so good I ask for seconds.

By the time Parisa's mom serves saffron tea, I'm full. "Can we have our tea on the rug?" Parisa asks. "Like at grandmother's house?"

We move from the table to the living room where Parisa's mom tosses a few pillows onto a colorful rug and we pile in and drink sweet, honeyed tea. It all feels so different but cozy. Parisa's parents don't seem that different from any other parents. Parisa's mom is wearing jeans and a yellow blouse and her dad is in khaki pants – no wait, *trousers* – and a golf shirt. Every now and then they'll say something to each other in their language. *Farsi*, is what Parisa told me, but other than that, they seem like a regular family who happens to drink sweet saffron tea on a beautiful, red floral rug.

"I really like your rug," I say.

"Thank you, Addie," Parisa's dad says. "Rugs are important in Iran. They tell the story of who you are and where you came from."

"So you brought this rug with you when you moved here?"

Everyone goes quiet.

"No," Parisa's mom answers after a moment. "We bought this rug here in London. It is nice, but not like the rugs back home." I want to ask why they didn't take their rugs with them, if they're so nice, but before I can Parisa's mom asks if I'd like to try saffron ice cream.

Would I ever! So far, everything they've set before me has been scrumptious and ice cream is something I'd never refuse.

"Your mom's super nice," I say some time later as Parisa and I watch purple stars generated by her light projector dance across the ceiling. We're laying on our backs on the top bunk in her and Jasmine's shared room.

"What is your mum like?" Parisa asks.

She thinks my dad and mom are divorced, I'm almost sure of it. I haven't lied exactly, I've just never told her the truth. When something awful happens to your mom, you don't always want to talk about it. "I don't remember her very well."

"When was the last time you saw her?"

"When I was nine."

Parisa props herself up halfway on her elbows and stares at me. "That's a long time."

"That's how old I was when she died."

"Oh."

That's what most kids say when they find out that my mom died. *Oh.*

The stars on the celling change to red. "What *do* you remember about her?"

I could tell Parisa about my mom's long brown hair and dark brown eyes that, people say, are just like mine, but when I close my eyes, an old memory smacks into me and what slips out is, "She smelled like buttered toast."

Parisa's going to laugh at me and I can't even blame her.

"Buttered toast? I guess that's a nice smell."

Parisa hasn't even cracked a smile so I go on. "I guess it's strange but when I was little, in the mornings, we'd eat toast together."

I remember climbing into Mom's lap and nestling into her fluffy blue robe, as the new day came alive outside. Mom would take a bite of toast, and then hold it out for me. Back and forth we'd crunch as crumbs sprinkled our legs and the sun rose in the sky.

My insides grow tight and achy. I try to shake away the memory.

I sit up and look at the photographs propped along the bookshelf. "Who's that?" I ask, pointing to a picture of Parisa and Jasmine and an older lady standing beside a green shrub with white blossoms.

"That's my grandmother and that's her house." She stretches out on her stomach, reaches for the photo, and studies it. "I know what you mean about smells and people. When I think of my grandmother, I smell jasmine."

I turn to her, confused. "Your grandma smells like your sister?"

Parisa looks bewildered. Then she begins to giggle. It starts as a trickle and grows into a stream, and soon she's caught up in a flood of laughter, trying to catch her breath. I have no idea what's so funny, but she *looks* funny, tears running down her red cheeks. I just have to join in.

"No, not Jasmine my sister," she finally gets out. "Jasmine the *flower*! My grandmother's house smelled like jasmine the *flower*!"

"Oh, that is different!"

She thumps the photo with her finger. "See these white flowers? *That* jasmine, not my sister!"

We laugh and laugh some more, and it feels so good I never want it to stop. After a while, it does. We lay our heads down again and dangle our feet over the railing of the bed. The stars on the ceiling bleed to purple. "Did you want to move to London?" I ask.

"No," Parisa says.

"But your parents came here for a job?"

"Not really." She lets out a sigh. "I miss having my own room, and I miss my rug."

"Why didn't you bring your rugs with you?"

"Because there wasn't time."

"Time for what?"

"To pack."

I look at her. "So when your parents decided to move, you just up and moved? Right away? You didn't pack anything?"

"We didn't *decide* to move." She props herself up on her elbows. "We *had* to move."

What does *that* mean? We're both the same age. It's not like we have much of a say in whether or not we get hauled away to a new country, but with Parisa there's more. We both miss home, but it sounds like no one in Parisa's family wanted to move. So why did they?

"Will you go back to Iran someday?"

Parisa jumps off the bunk. Replaces the photograph of her grandmother beside the jasmine plant. "We can't go back. We're not allowed."

I try to think of something funny to say to bring back those laughing girls from five minutes ago, but I can't even think of a good knock-knock joke. Laughter is a funny thing. It can bubble up like soda pop and fizzle out just as quickly. As much as you may want to hold on to it, when it's gone, it's gone.

That next time I have tea with Lillian, I tell her about Parisa's family not being allowed back into Iran. "I don't get it. Why aren't they?"

Lilian fills the yellow teapot with boiling water. "Because not all countries are free. In Iran, the regime controls the people through endless rules."

"What kind of rules?"

Lilian sets out two cups. "Reporters and artists aren't free to express their opinions, people are forbidden to change or share their religion, and women – well, women face the most difficulty. Many activities you and I take for granted are outlawed."

"Like what?"

"Showing their hair and skin. Riding a bike. Singing, dancing, and talking too loudly in public..."

"Wait a minute. Girls aren't allowed to dance? I wouldn't be allowed to tap dance?"

"Not outside your home."

"That's crazy. I'd just break the rules."

Lilian studies me. "An easy boast for someone who isn't in danger."

"What happens if you break the rules?"

"You go to prison. Or much worse."

Lilian pours the tea. She adds sugar and milk to mine and a splash of milk to hers.

"You'd think Parisa would be glad to leave Iran."

"No one wants to live under such an oppressive government, but Iran is Parisa's home," Lilian reminds me. "I'm sure she misses it just like you miss America."

"I think they left because of their religion."

"Quite possible."

I think of Parisa and Jasmine and girls far away who aren't allowed to dance, who have to be super careful about following the rules so they don't wind up in jail. "It's not fair."

"Indeed." Lilian hands me my cup. "Have some tea."

I dutifully take a sip of tea and we fall quiet. Running out of words when I'm with Lilian isn't as awkward anymore. Sometimes it's kind of nice not to have to think of something to say.

Earl Grey struts in and parks himself next to Lilian's chair. I reach my hand out, hoping he'll come closer and let me pet him. He only looks at me in contempt, turns up his squashed nose, and saunters away.

Lilian stands and steps out of the kitchen. She returns with an envelope which she sets on the table in front of me. "Your father has already granted his permission."

"Permission for what?"

I open the envelope and find two tickets. "What's this?"

"Tickets to *42nd Street*. It's a musical playing in the West End."

"Cool! What's the *West End*?"

"The West End is London's theatre district. Similar to Broadway in New York."

I peer at the tickets again. "I've never heard of *42nd Street*."

"It's marvellous. Big flashy songs and copious amounts of dancing."

"Tap dancing?"

She smiles. "Tap dancing galore. Dress smart."

I know by now she doesn't mean wear my school uniform.

6

There's an empty spot across from the lady in the green hat. I quickly slide onto the worn upholstery patterned with pink, green, and yellow rectangles. The lady glances up from the book she's holding and nods, a slight smile playing at her lips. We've never been this close before.

My hair is dripping all over the dingy linoleum floor that's designed to look like it's covered in confetti. As if we're at a party instead of trapped in a metal container squished next to soggy strangers.

You know what the opposite of fun is? Dragging yourself to school on a rainy London morning. When I flew from the apartment this morning, the blue sky was dotted with white cotton clouds, so I didn't think to grab an umbrella. But London weather yo-yos from sun to rain to hail to sun again, sometimes all within five minutes. A few steps outside this morning and *bam!* Downpour.

Days like this make me miss my old life more than ever. Right now, riding in the car with Dad all cozy and dry seems like a dream, even with his cringy singing.

I wring out the ends of my hair. Water droplets smatter my knees and I huff in irritation.

The lady smiles slightly as she sympathetically looks me over from head to toe. She's not the teensiest bit wet. What's more, her hair is perfectly behaved. How does she do it? She returns her attention to her book and I continue to fuss with my hair and secretly watch her.

She sits tall. Back straight, feet pressed together. I'm slouching I realize. Slowly I straighten up and bring Mary closer to Jane until they're sitting side by side.

As we rumble to the next stop, I keep a lookout for Parisa. We decided if we both try to board the front of the train, we might find each other. That's the plan anyway. A mob of passengers squeezes in but no Parisa or Jasmine. An old man is the last to hobble on before the train whisks us away.

The lady in the green hat's eyes rest pointedly upon me.

What? What does she want?

She glances at the old man, then back at me, then raises her eyebrows as if to say, *what are you going to do here?*

Right! I spring up. "Would you like to sit down?"

The old man mumbles something and lowers himself into my seat.

The lady smiles.

I grin back.

When she and I both exit at Earl's Court Station, I can't help wondering where she goes. Does she have a job? A family? I could follow her. Just for a little while. I take two steps after her until someone grabs my arm.

"Found you!"

I smile, glad to see Parisa, but when I turn back around… "She's gone."

"Who's gone?" asks Parisa.

I strain to spot the cheery green hat, but it's nowhere in sight. "No one important," I say, which is not true.

I may not know who the lady in the green hat is, but I know, deep down, she is important. Not to be ignored. There's a reason she keeps showing up, especially when the day is rainy, and my thoughts are dark, and I'm longing for life to go back to how it once was.

It's the night of the musical and it's me versus my hair. I brush and brush until my scalp burns, but my frizz flies everywhere. I grab a portion and wrangle it into a half ponytail which ends up lumpy and crooked. With a growl, I pitch my brush across the room.

Dad pops his head into my room. "Everything okay?"

He retrieves the brush and crosses over to me and tries to brush the loose part of my hair. He's trying to be nice, but he's making it worse. "Dad, *stop!*"

He drops the brush on my bed. "Just trying to help."

I tug out the hairband, shake out my mane. A plain old ponytail will have to do for the West End.

Dad sits down on the edge of the bed. "Girls' night out, huh?"

"Lilian's not a girl, Dad. She's old."

"She used to be a girl."

"I guess."

Dad absently watches me wriggle in my small gold hoop earrings. He's entered the sad trance, and I know he's thinking about her. I don't want to make him feel any sadder by talking about Mom, but we rarely do anymore – not like when she first died – even though sometimes it feels as if she's here, an invisible barrier between us. Especially when having a mom around would help a lot. Like right now when I can almost feel the gentle tug of her fingers coaxing my hair into two tidy French braids. Mom used to braid my hair at least once a week.

"Five more minutes and you should be knocking at Lilian's door," Dad says and exits my room.

Right. On to shoes. I'm wearing the purple dress Aunt Becky bought me, but my dressy shoes pinch like tweezers and I'm not about to let squished toes spoil my night. Mary and Jane would look alright with this outfit, but no way am I going to wear school shoes for a night out in the city!

I rummage through my shoe pile. My lime green canvas sneakers seem to be waving *pick me, pick me!* so I slip them on. They don't match the purple dress at all. But somehow it works. The opposite colors look good together.

Impulsively, I reach up and attempt to smooth my unruly hair but then remember something. The gold ribbon! I drop to the floor, slide out my box, and pull out the glittery ribbon that Aunt Becky tied around the macaroni and cheese boxes she sent.

I undo the ponytail, tuck the gold ribbon underneath my hair, and tie a nice fat bow right at the top of my head. The wires in the cloth allow me to shape the ribbon just so and the long ends trail down my hair like gold highlights.

There. Better.

"Smashing," is what Lilian says when I show up at her door minutes later. She owns a car but never drives into the city, so we take the Underground.

Riding the Tube feels different on a Saturday night. During the week, people stand nose to nose, frowning at their phones, as solemn as a library. But now, everyone seems happy and chatty, as if we're all going to a party and I'm invited. At one stop, a woman bursts into the carriage with a huge bouquet of balloons and down at the end, a man with earbuds, closed eyes, and a tuxedo perches his fingers in midair and practices an invisible piano.

Lilian and I hop off at Leicester Square. Lit up billboards and music from street performers fill the night sky. "Don't bother with that production," Lillian critiques as we scurry past theatre after theatre "but this musical, this one is stunning."

Finally, we arrive at our theatre and settle into our seats. The lights dim. A hidden orchestra rumbles into life. The curtain creeps up and for a little while, all you can see are feet. Dozens and dozens of feet. All tapping in perfect step. Then the curtain lifts all the way to reveal a stage bursting with dazzling lights and beaming dancers wearing every shade of the rainbow, their bodies synchronized like one big happy machine.

I lean forward. How I should have worn my tap shoes!

The show is about Peggy, a girl who moved to New York to become a famous tap dancer. And Lilian's right, there's tons of dancing, and singing too. I grow a little sleepy in the second act – too many romantic parts – but during the final scene, when all the dancers burst onto stage and shuffle-ball-step as if they've only just begun, I wake right up.

The music soars, the curtain falls, and we the audience explode into cheers. Our turn to act like one big happy machine.

"Not bad. Not bad at all," Lilian says when the applause dissolves.

I throw my arms around her neck. "That was the best show ever!"

She wobbles a little and pats my back. "Alright now, alright. Let's get you home before the Tube is overflowing with barmy crackers."

On the ride home, I'm just beginning to nod off when the train jerks to a stop. The engineer announces over the loudspeaker that we've encountered an unexpected delay and he's sorry for any inconvenience. We wait. People sigh and shift. I open my small pink purse and help myself to a mint. I offer one to Lilian, but she says no thank you.

A few minutes pass.

The engineer apologizes again. We should be moving shortly, he promises.

Lilian clicks her tongue. "*Shortly*. They don't know the meaning of the word."

More minutes pass.

I twist around to look out the window behind me. There's nothing to see but darkness. Nothing but the dismal walls of the tunnel we're stuck in that's buried deep below the city like a coffin.

What if we're trapped here for hours? Forever caged on the Piccadilly line with its mangy upholstery and rattling air vents? Lilian's right. We should be moving forward.

That's the whole point of the Tube, the reason you put up with the bumpy ride: to get to some place better. Like a West End show. Or school. Home.

But here we are, caught in limbo land, stuck on a train going nowhere. With seats that seem to be growing scratcher by the minute and walls that seem to be closing in by the second and if we don't start moving soon, I might scream. As if things couldn't get any worse, the lights flicker off.

Lilian heaves a sigh. "Such a bother."

The faces surrounding me are grey and ghostly. I lean forward and peer down our murky carriage, all the way through the back window and into the carriage behind us.

My heart catches in my throat. In the dimness I make out a familiar profile: a figure in a rounded hat with a tilted brim. The silhouetted head tips up and slowly turns my way and although I can't make out the eyes, I sense they're zeroing in straight on me.

Just then the lights flicker on. The train jolts forward, startling me backwards in my seat.

We're moving!

I glance back at the carriage behind us. No woman. No hat. Did I imagine her? It's a crazy thought but did *she* somehow get us unstuck?

7

My tie has run away.

I've looked everywhere. Under my bed, in the laundry, even in the kitchen cupboards although no way could my tie have ended up between the frosted flakes and granola. I slide my hand between the couch cushions. Not there. I throw off all the coats from their hooks by the front door. Nothing. I rifle through the catch-all basket we keep in the corner. No tie! I've spent so much time searching I'm now going to be late for school! I have no other choice but to fly out the door without it.

"Did you leave it in your locker?" Parisa asks as we jostle along on the District line.

"No. It's *nowhere*. It's just vanished."

Victoria straightens her own tie which is just plain mean. "Ties don't simply disappear."

"Well, mine did."

"You ought to take better care of your things," Victoria admonishes.

"And you ought to –"

"What do you plan to do?" Parisa interrupts before I can finish the insult.

I shrug. "Go to class without a tie."

"That's not a plan, Addie," Victoria says.

"Well what else am I supposed to do?" I snap back, wringing the safety pole extra tightly so my hands don't yank her tie from her neck and toss it out the window. "It's just a stupid tie. It's not like wearing one causes our brains to work any better. If I behave well and do my best, maybe nobody will notice."

Victoria shakes her head. "You're delusional."

Someone *does* notice. Not in French class because the replacement teacher had bigger problems to tackle, and not in PE because we change out of our uniforms, but in Math when Sir towers over my desk.

"Addie Brown, you appear to have forgotten your tie."

Oliver Ridley turns around and studies my tie-less self.

"I didn't forget," I clarify.

"No? Well, then. If it's not around your neck, where is it?"

"I have absolutely no idea."

Sir exhales nosily through his nose. "Such disrespect is the pathway to detention."

Disrespect? I wasn't trying to be disrespectful; I was telling the truth. I haven't *forgotten* my tie. My tie is the only thing I've been thinking about all day. I just can't find it.

"You cannot attend lessons without a tie."

"But Sir, why not? I promise I can do the work just as well without a tie as I can with a tie."

You would think that a Math teacher would appreciate my logic. You would think, but you'd be wrong.

Sir fixes his eyes on me, then strides to his desk, scrawls something on a slip of paper, and holds it up. "Addie Brown, go to reception and sort yourself out. Then after school, go straight to detention."

With Oliver and the whole class watching, I plod to the front of the room, Mary and Jane loudly sounding their protest against the tile floor.

A boy called Peter smirks as I pass by. "Maybe you left your tie in America along with half of your brain."

Banished, I take the yellow paper from Sir and turn myself in at reception. The lady at the counter sets down the phone and looks up at me. "Yes?"

"I... lost... my... my..."

"Your tie? Come on then, let's get you sorted." She motions for me to follow her to the room behind the office. "Was it labelled? Is your name on it?"

Another slip-up. "No."

"Hm. Well, that might make it a wee bit more difficult to track down but with a bit of luck, we'll find something for you in the trusty lost and found." She kneels down and plunges her hand into a big box. "Come on then, don't let me have all the fun," she says with a grin.

I crouch down and dig through the items. A bookbag. A pair of sneakers. A leopard print bucket hat which I twirl around my finger.

"Isn't that a dandy? And what's this?" She extracts a hot pink zebra shirt and holds it against her blouse. "Are we running a zoo or a school!"

I giggle.

We continue to hunt.

"Aha!" She triumphantly holds up and examines a tie. "No label so it's yours. Perhaps it truly *is* yours." She smooths out the wrinkles and hands it to me.

I thank her and secure it to my collar. I'm grateful she found it, but couldn't it have taken a little longer? Searching for lost things is a whole lot better than sitting in a classroom with mean boys and an unsympathetic teacher.

"I did tell you," Victoria reminds me at lunch after I spill the story. "I did say wearing a tie was essential."

I slurp my milk extra loud and glare at her.

"At least you found one," Parisa says.

I open my lunch bag to find a banana. Only a banana. Rats! Dad and I were so distracted looking for my tie, we never finished packing my lunch. "I forgot my sandwich."

"Oh Addie, really," Victoria scolds. "First your tie, now your lunch. Did you forget your History homework as well?"

"No."

She holds out half of her sandwich. "Here."

But I don't need her gorgeous looking ham and cheese sandwich, I've got a banana, a bruised, beat up, tired looking banana. I turn up my nose and take my time peeling my little lunch. "No thank you."

Victoria thrusts the sandwich closer. "Don't be a nitwit. Take it. I've packed enough to share with anyone in need."

"I'm not *in need*." I take an enormous bite of mush to prove it. No way am I going to feed her smugness by giving her the pleasure of helping poor forgetful Addie. She could offer me an Aldo's pizza and I'd still refuse. I think.

Victoria purses her lips and retracts the sandwich.

"Shall we meet by the big tree after school again?" Parisa asks, scooting her lunch tray closer in case I want anything.

"Yes! Let's!" Ellie says.

I help myself to one of Parisa's carrot batons. "I can't. I got detention."

Ellie's eyes grow wide. "You got *detention*?"

"Oh, Addie it's only your first term," Victoria says.

"What will your dad say?" Parisa asks.

"Maybe he won't know."

"They call your parents," Ellie says. "My brother gets detention all the time. He says it's utterly dismal!"

Ellie's brother is right. The only thing you're allowed to do in detention is sit. Not read, not do your homework, not fold your arms on your desk and rest your head. Only *sit*.

Fifty minutes lasts forever. When my sentence is over, I drag myself to the station, board the train, and huddle close to the door where I stare at the reflection of the miserable looking girl with frizzy hair in the grimy window.

It's damp and dreary. In Wisconsin, people are enjoying a crisp, bright fall. I picture the red palm-sized leaves of our maple tree in our old backyard, dazzling brighter than the rest of the trees in the neighborhood; the leaves dry and drifting down to be raked into big, crunchy piles, perfect for jumping in and destroying.

I see all of my friends jumping in and out of mounds of leaves and burrowing through piles like squirrels until bits of leaves stick in their hair and ears and mouth; until they can actually taste fall. Then the grown-ups haul the leaf piles away or set little fires and carefully guard them while curls of smoke drift to the sky.

Fall in Wisconsin is happening without me.

Maybe Peter is right. Maybe parts of me, like my brain, are stuck back in America, like I'm a human jigsaw puzzle with missing pieces. Important pieces you need to make the whole picture, the whole me. Lauren and Aunt Becky. My old school and my neighborhood. My yard. My tree. My room. My life. My mom.

My throat tightens and tears spring to my eyes. I tip my head down. Stare at the floor. Swallow hard. But it's too late. The tears fall. One drops on Jane, creating a tiny perfect circle on the shiny leather of my shoe.

Please, please, please, let no one from school be on this train.

I let go of the safety handle to wipe my eyes. The train lurches and I lose my balance. Prepared to apologize to whoever I might have bumped into, I glance over my shoulder and gasp. It's her. Standing right behind me. Clear even through my blurry vision.

The lady in the green hat doesn't say a word, but her eyes look as sad as I feel, as if she can read my thoughts, view the pictures in my head. As if she's missing something, too.

The train stops. I hoist my backpack onto my shoulders, the lady's gaze still fixed on me. Her lips part, as if she's about to say something, but this is my stop, and even though a ridiculous part of me wants to tuck myself into her chest and cry, I can't. I step off the train.

From the platform, I turn around. She's still watching me, intently, and presses her hand against the glass window. I duck my head to fumble in my pockets for a tissue. By the time I wipe my drippy nose and look up again, she is gone.

I trudge home. The wind blows harshly against my blazer that now feels thin and flimsy. When I open the door to my apartment, I hear a woman's voice: "Of course, I'm worried about her."

Aunt Becky.

My heart soars. For one tiny, delicious moment, I think she's here, in the flesh, waiting in the next room. But it's only technology. Aunt Becky's face and voice may be transmitting through Dad's computer, but the rest of her, the huggable her, is an ocean away.

"Addie's doing okay," Dad says. "You've got to give us time. We haven't been here that long."

I freeze where I am. Dad hasn't heard me come in. From where I'm standing, I see a sliver of his back in the kitchen.

"Calvin, you know I've never been fully supportive of this move."

"Look, I don't know what else to say, Becs. We needed a change."

"*You* needed a change. Addie's nearly a teenager. *She* needs consistency."

"I don't know what else to tell you. I had to get out of Wisconsin. At least for a while. Go someplace where every sight and sound doesn't remind me of Isabella."

"But what about Addie?" Aunt Becky says, her voice rising. "What if the best thing for her is to stay close to the family she's got?"

Silence. Then Dad's broken voice. "I'm doing my best."

"I know you are. I'm just concerned that all of these changes might be too much for her."

"Haven't I done okay single-parenting these past three years? I haven't done everything right, but we've survived, haven't we?"

"You've been a rockstar, Cal. I'm just worried about my niece. And you."

Dad shifts in his seat and I panic. I shut the door hard, pretending like if I've just stepped in. "I'm home!" I yell extra cheerfully as I kick off Mary and Jane.

"There's my girl!" Aunt Becky says when I step into the kitchen. "How was school?"

"Okay."

"What was the best part of your day?"

Today? Nothing. No best part. I could tell her about my missing tie and my banishment and detention, but Dad looks so weary that I don't want to give her another reason to worry about me and be angry at him.

"I sit with some girls at lunch. They're okay."

This prompts Aunt Becky to play twenty questions. What are their names? What do they look like? What do we talk about? What do we eat? I describe the four of us, bossy Victoria, funny Ellie, and kind Parisa. When it's time to hang up to eat dinner, I feel a little better. Not happy, but okay.

"I'm here for you, girl," Aunt Becky says. "You know that, right?"

I do. Aunt Becky has always loved me by an extra dose because I'm a girl and she and Uncle Chad have three boys. Even when mom was around, Aunt Becky always showered me with pink, sparkly things and loved to take me shopping and play princess dress-up even more than I did.

"Thanks, Aunt Becky."

"Miss you like crazy," she says.

I miss her too, more than ever. Life may be going on back home without me, but I haven't been completely forgotten. Not by Aunt Becky, at least.

Before I go to bed, I find a black Sharpie and carefully print my name on the inside tag of my runaway tie. There. If the thing ever strays again, everyone will know who it belongs to.

8

Parisa and I are sifting through craft ideas on her iPad one afternoon when Jasmine enters the bedroom wrapped in a bathrobe with a towel on her head. "Oh," she says when she sees me. "Hi Addie. I didn't know you were here."

She blots her hair with the towel, combs it through, and spritzes it with something that smells like oranges. Then she tosses her head upside down and scrunches chunks of hair in her fists. When she flips right side up, her hair falls past her shoulders in gorgeous waves.

"I wish my hair did that," I say.

"Maybe it would."

"I don't think so. My hair just sticks up all over no matter how much I brush it."

Jasmine turns and studies me. "Maybe you shouldn't brush it. Maybe your hair wants to be curly. Come here."

I can't scramble off the bed fast enough.

Jasmine sits me down in the desk chair and runs her fingers through my mop. "If you grew it out longer it might lay down nicer but for now let's try this." She finds a blue plastic bottle from the shelf and starts spraying my head.

"What is that?" I ask.

"Water."

Parisa runs out for a fresh towel and covers my shoulders like I'm at a beauty salon. Jasmine combs through my damp hair, spritzes me with the orange stuff, and begins to scrunch.

"Okay," she says. "Now stand up and flip your head upside down."

I obey.

She spritzes and scrunches some more and tells me to flip right side up again.

When I do Parisa gasps.

I see myself in the mirror and yelp. It's huge! I'm a crazed lion!

"Jasmine, what have you done?" Parisa cries, trying to smooth down the disaster with the palms of her hands.

"Everyone stay calm! I can fix this." Jasmine throws the towel over my head so I can't see.

She and Parisa lead me to the bathroom and douse my hair at the sink. Then they towel-dry, comb through, spritz, spritz, spritz, but this time, instead of hanging me upside down, Jasmine gently scrunches and twists sections of hair around her finger.

"There," she finally says. I open my eyes, one at a time and peek in the mirror.

No more out of control lion's mane. It's curly. Controlled.

"I like it," I say.

"See?" Jasmine says proudly. "Your hair wants to be curly. Let it be curly."

The more I examine it, the more I like it. I take a mental picture of the hair product. The sooner I can get my hands on this magic potion the better.

I beg Dad to buy me a bottle as soon as he collects me but for now, my plan is to keep the curls for as long as possible. If that means wrapping my hair in cling film and covering my head in a plastic bag before taking a shower, so be it. That night I shower and dry off quickly then carefully unwrap my curls so I can present them to Lauren when we FaceTime tonight.

Dad sets me up with the laptop and I call Lauren as planned. It rings and rings, but she doesn't pick up. I end the call and try again.

Nothing.

Did she forget? Is she with Madison? What if she's off doing something super fun and exciting without me?

I return the laptop to Dad, kiss him goodnight, and go to bed determined not to toss and turn away my curls in my sleep. I hardly sleep a wink but it's worth it. In the morning my hair looks almost as good as it did the day before.

In Math, when Oliver Ridley turns around to hand me a worksheet, I give my head a little toss. Oliver studies me like I'm a Math problem.

But good old Ellie comes through. "Ooh!" she coos at lunch. "Your hair looks brilliant!"

"Thanks! Parisa's sister did it."

"You allowed Parisa's sister to cut your hair?" Victoria asks.

"She didn't cut it. She *styled* it. And here. Smell." I lean across the table so Victoria can get a whiff of orange.

After school the four of us journey to the station together with Oliver, Peter, and another boy trailing us. We board the train and huddle by the door, our backs toward the boys.

"I simply *must* find a new black dress," Victoria says. She's been carrying on and on about getting ready for her upcoming violin recital. "I've outgrown the one I wore last season so Mum's taking me shopping on Oxford Street."

"Ooh, I love Oxford Street at Christmas time," Ellie says. "We go to see the lights every year."

"Don't be silly, Ellie. I can't wait until Christmas. I need a dress now."

I toss my head from side to side, savoring how my curls bounce against my shoulders.

"Watch it!" one of the boys behind us warns.

I only half listen as Victoria prattles on. Every now and then, I twist a section of hair around my finger, just like Jasmine taught me.

I'm working my way to the back of my tresses when suddenly my fingers come across a hard, sticky mass. *What in the world...?* And then it hits me.

I whip around. "Who put gum in my hair?"

The trio of boys says nothing.

"*Who* put *gum* in my *hair*?" I demand louder, my face on fire.

Peter looks smug. "Don't know what you're going on about."

Victoria examines the back of my head and gasps. "You beasts!" she scolds. "You ought to be ashamed of yourselves!"

I want to hug her.

Peter tips his chin up and smirks. "Anything could have happened, with you tossing your head about like that."

The train stops at Earl's Court. The doors open but my feet don't move.

"Come on," Parisa urges, pulling my hand. "Addie, we've got to change trains."

But I can't leave this train. Those smug little weasels can't get away with this! Fists clenched, I glare at horrible Peter, my mind searching for words to hurl at him. "You'll… You'll be sorry you messed with me!"

"Oh no," Peter says flatly. "I'm terrified."

Parisa takes me by my shoulders and steers me off the carriage seconds before the doors shut.

"My brother put gum in my hair once," Ellie divulges as we make our way along the platform. "We had to use peanut butter to loosen it."

Victoria scrutinizes the damage again. "Your mum will have to cut it out," she concludes before she and Ellie head for the exit.

Parisa and I find two empty seats on the District line. "It's really stuck in there," she says, picking at the lump before we reach her stop and she leaves me in my misery all by myself. I journey the rest of the way without touching a strand.

I shuffle home. Dad works late tonight. He's arranged for Lillian to be "on call", in case of an emergency on the few nights he's not there when I get home. Is this an emergency? What would Lilian do if I knocked on her door with a wad of gum in my hair? She'd help, but it would cost me. A look. A lecture. I'm at high school, I tell myself. I can handle this on my own.

At home I find a comb and try to wiggle the teeth into the gummy patch, but the gob doesn't budge. If anything, I might be making it worse.

I'm allergic to peanuts. No peanut butter in this house to rescue me.

I'm out of options. I find the scissors in a kitchen drawer. I march to my room. Standing in front of my mirror, I grip the gummy mass with my left hand, and the scissors with my right. I can't see the back of my head so before I lose my nerve, I shut my eyes, open the mouth of the scissors and...

Snip. Snaaap.

I open my eyes. On the floor at my feet lays what looks like a small brown mouse. Is that really my hair? I feel the back of my head, grab my small mirror, and examine my handiwork. I feel sick. The jagged gap is worse than I had imagined.

I moan, the sound of it creepy and loud in the empty apartment with no one around to help. No Dad to fix the problem, or older sister to advise, or Mom to wipe my tears and tell me everything's going to be alright. If Mom were here, none of this would have happened in the first place. If Mom were alive, we wouldn't have moved to London. If Mom hadn't died, I'd be back in America where I belong. With hair. With Lauren. With a dad *and* a mom.

I begin to cry. Hard. No tissues either. I reach for my blanket and wipe my nose on the soft fleece.

When the tears ease up, I take a shower, any hope to hold on to my beautiful curls swirling down the drain. I put on clean pajamas and curl up on the couch to wait for Dad. When I hear his key in the lock I don't get up or holler hello. I stay on the couch, tucked in a miserable ball.

"Hey there Addie girl," Dad calls from the kitchen.

He goes to the freezer and takes out a box of fish fingers and a bag of peas. I sigh, loud enough for him to hear. I'm sick of frozen fish and peas but that's exactly what kind of day this is.

With some effort, I haul myself to the kitchen.

"School okay?" Dad arranges the fish fingers on a baking tray.

He doesn't notice my pajamas or my wet hair. He doesn't notice the hole in the back of my head. Shouldn't he notice? Isn't that his job? It's only six o'clock and I never take a shower this early.

I sit at the kitchen counter and prop my face in my hands. "Do we have to have fish tonight?"

"It's all we have at the moment."

I groan.

"I know, I know. I need to start a grocery order," Dad says. "Hey, unless you want to learn to do it? You might think it's fun ordering groceries online."

"No! I don't want to order groceries! That's what *grown-ups* are supposed to do!" I stomp off to my room and slam the door so hard my mirror rattles.

After fifteen or so minutes Dad raps on my door. He says the food is ready and that I don't have to help with the grocery order. He was only asking.

I come out. We heap our plates and settle ourselves in the living room where we watch a show about fish that swim freely in Australia's Great Barrier Reef. Maybe the fish I'm nibbling came from Australia. Maybe they used to swim around in that big, beautiful, colorful ocean until one day they were captured and shipped to gloomy London where they ended up on my plate.

I guess nobody gets to decide what kind of life they're going to have. Not even fish.

9

The only way to hide my cosmetic catastrophe is with two barrettes and a tight, low ponytail. Looks like I'm doomed to ponytails for the rest of my life.

In Math, when Oliver turns around to hand me a worksheet, he doesn't seem the tiniest bit sorry. He may not have been the one to put the gum in my hair, but he was there. He should have stopped horrible Peter. And he should at least *look* sorry. I take the worksheets without a glance. I turn up my nose and pretend he's invisible.

At lunchtime the girls have a million questions.

"Did you get it out?" Parisa asks.

"Did you use peanut butter?" Ellie wants to know.

"I used scissors."

"Oh Addie," Victoria says. "You didn't cut it yourself, did you?"

"I had to."

"Let's see it," Ellie says.

"No way Jose," I say.

"Addie, you can't wear a ponytail forever," Victoria admonishes.

"Watch me." I look up from my sandwich to see Peter sauntering toward us.

What if my foot just happened to thrust itself out and Peter just happened to trip, causing his tray to soar through the air, and meat sauce rain down on him like red paint. Wouldn't that be something? But Mary and Jane, cowards that they are, remain meekly under the table.

"Hiya Frizz," horrible Peter says as he passes our table. "Got any gum?"

Later, I try to call Lauren. Again. She doesn't pick up. Again. What's going on with her? Her visit is only weeks away! We've got plans to make!

She couldn't be avoiding me, could she?

The following day my English teacher assigns us an essay. It's not due until November, she says, but she wants to give us plenty of time to think. Not only do we have to write an essay about a memory, using lots of details and comparisons, but we have to read our essay in front of the whole class. Ugh.

After lessons, Parisa and I brainstorm what to write about.

"You could write about when you left Iran," I suggest, pulling my backpack from my jam-packed locker so fiercely I think I might have torn the stitching.

Lilian has warned me not to pry. Respect Parisa's privacy, she advised. But I can't help hoping the mystery of how and why Parisa's family came to London will be revealed through an English assignment.

"No, I'm going to write about when I turned nine and my mom took Jasmine and me to Kish Island."

"What's that?"

"An island in Iran. With the most beautiful beach you could ever imagine, and I got to go swimming for the first time."

"The first time you went swimming at a beach was when you were nine?"

Parisa looks at her shoes. "Girls aren't allowed to swim at most beaches. Unless they have a women's section."

I slam my locker shut. Another unfair rule.

"It was loads of fun," Parisa continues as we start down the hall. "We ate ice cream and jumped in the waves and played in the sand for hours."

We've almost reached the end of the hall when Parisa surprises me by turning into a classroom. "You're not coming?"

"I have Maths club," she says.

We say goodbye and I head to the station.

When I change trains at Earl's Court, I think of Parisa swimming at the beach for the first time. Summers are made for water. Last summer, Lauren and I would beg her mom to take us swimming nearly every other day. Cool water, warm sun, soft blanket beneath you, lazing around with someone you love.

Snapshots in my mind piece together and a memory rises to the surface. Sun. A blanket. Books. My mom.

I'm very little, on a blanket in our sunny backyard, and nestled very close to Mom. We're surrounded by picture books and sharing a bowl of green grapes. The grapes are tart, the books are colorful, our feet are bare, the sun is warm, and we are happy.

That's it. That's all I remember. Not much to it. Hardly enough material to whip into a three-paragraph essay, but I know for certain that I haven't embellished a dream or a photograph; it's a true memory. It's just been buried underneath all the other things my brain is supposed to remember. Stumbling across it now is like finding an old letter in a jumbled closet.

But it doesn't change anything. Mom's still not here. This memory in the sunshine doesn't replace the memory of the night two officers showed up at our house when I was nine. When life as I knew it came to a screeching halt.

My throat grows prickly but I will not start crying again. As the train crawls into the station, I squeeze my eyes shut.

When I open them, I spot her. On the platform. Sitting on a bench as if she's waiting for me. The lady in the green hat sees me, opens the small book she's holding, and scribbles something down. Then she rips out the page and, looking directly at me, holds it up. She folds the paper once and tucks it between the slats of the bench.

It's for me. She's written a note for me.

The lady stands up, tips her hat in my direction, and strides away.

The carriage doors sweep open. I have five seconds to decide. Five seconds before the heavy train door separates me from her, me from the note.

Five, four, three…

Beep beep beep! I bolt to my feet and leap to the platform. I grab the slip of paper and sit down. With trembling fingers, I open it:

It's a bumpy ride, I know. Chin up. You're going to make it. You're going to be alright.

I glance up, searching for the splash of green. I rush to the stairs and join the herd of commuters climbing up and out. Where did she go? How does she know I'm going to be alright?

I weave in and out of people, straining to get ahead to find her, but too many obstacles stand in my way. A mother tugging her little boy. A yapping dog on a leash. A group of older, scary looking teenagers. I want to scream for the world to stop. If everyone and everything could just stop moving for a second, maybe I could find the lady in the green hat, sort out who she is and discover what she wants from me.

But what would I say to her?

What more might she say to me?

I make it to the top of the stairs, caught in the current of commuters flowing toward the exit. But no lady. No green hat. She couldn't have vanished into thin air, could she?

Bodies rush around me. Trains roar back and forth. Life keeps pulsing in this buzzing hive but the lady in the green hat is nowhere to be seen. I look at the note in my hand. I'm not going crazy. She was here.

"Do you need any help, love?"

I turn around, hopeful. But it's not her. It's only an older woman in a raincoat. I'm blocking traffic and pull off to the side.

"No. Thanks. I'm alright."

The woman smiles and continues to the exit.

I turn around. Plod down the steps. Back at the platform I plop down on the bench, in the exact spot where the lady sat and wonder what would it be like to be grown up, to have life all figured out? What would it be like to be her?

That night before bed I shake out my ponytail and feel the bald patch. No miraculous regrowth of hair. I wander out of my bedroom and find Dad at the table, hunched over his laptop.

"Dad?"

"Hm?

"Could you please get me a bottle of *Citrus Curl?*"

"What's that?"

"It's a spray for hair."

"Yeah, sure. I can get you some hair spray."

"No, not hair spray. *Citrus Curl*!"

He finally looks up. "Okay, Addie. I'll look for it tomorrow."

"Promise?"

"Promise."

But the next day? No *Citrus Curl*. And the day after that? Nothing. Apparently, there are a million other things more pressing than tracking down a life-changing hair product. It's hard being a kid. How do you explain to your dad that something that seems unimportant to him, means all the world to you?

Later that night, Lauren calls me back. It's about time!

I nestle into my bed with the laptop and feel instantly better. Lauren will listen to me gripe about Peter and we can plan out what we're going to do and where we're going to go. When she visits in person, it'll be just like old times.

"You got them, right? The airline tickets!"

A funny look clouds her face. "Well... No."

"What are you waiting for?"

She starts picking at her fingernails. "That's what I have to talk to you about."

"Okay. What?"

"I can't come."

I haven't heard her right. "What are you talking about? Before I left, your mom said it would work for the two of you to come to London that week..."

"She said it *might* work. But it doesn't."

Joy seeps out of me like air hisses out of a pin-pricked balloon. I feel like I can't breathe. "Why not?"

She shrugs. "Because of my mom's schedule. Because I've got stuff going on."

What could be more important than visiting me in London? "What stuff?"

"I don't know. Just… stuff. Piano lessons and school I shouldn't miss and Madison's birthday…"

There it is. The real reason. She's choosing Madison. Over me. I've been replaced. A door inside of me slams hard. "I thought we were best friends."

"We are!"

No, I want to shriek. Best friends are there for each other. Best friends visit when one of them moves to a strange, alien city. Best friends don't become best friends with someone else just because you're far apart. Parisa springs to mind, but I push the thought away. That's different. It's not the same thing. I haven't given up on Lauren like Lauren is giving up on me.

We're both silent.

"I'm sorry," she says after a while, "but my mom just doesn't think it's a good time to go."

So what? I tell myself. Who needs her? Not me. I don't say a word.

"I gotta go," she says after a long time.

"Yeah, me too."

I slam the laptop shut as hard as I can.

10

Tuesday tea with Lilian. Rain spits against the window. Books litter the kitchen table. Lilian's showing me photographs of Egyptian artifacts in a big book about the British Museum. When she asked about school, I mentioned we were learning about Ancient Egypt. Apparently, she took it as a sign that I'm eager to know more. I'm not.

"And this is Ramses II, one of the greatest pharaohs in history," Lilian says, pointing to a statue of a man with a mischievous smirk and no arms.

Earl Grey is lounging under the table. Every now and then I wiggle my fingers, hoping to entice him to play. He only glowers.

Lilian turns the page. "The British Museum houses thousands of Egyptian antiquities. Have you not been? Has your father taken you?"

I sigh. "I don't remember. We've been to the museum with the big whale skeleton..."

"The Natural History Museum."

"...and the one with all the paintings with the stone lions outside."

"The National Portrait Gallery. Good, good. Might I suggest the British Museum for your next outing. It boasts the very best of Britain's treasure."

I turn away to watch the rain-tears wobble down the window. Who cares about museums and artifacts? Did the pharaoh of Egypt's best friend ever bail on him? Did he ever get gum stuck in his hair and have to cut it out by himself? Probably not.

"Are you unwell Addie? You look rather pallid."

"I'm okay."

I hear the book close with a gentle thud. "Well, you've not lived in the city for long. No sense trying to fit a thousand years of history into your first three months, I suppose." She falls quiet. Then, "How are you getting on at school?"

"Fine."

"How is your friend Parisa?"

"Fine."

"Do you get on with your classmates, then?"

"Mostly. Except for some of the boys."

"Boys can be silly creatures."

I make a snorting sound and cross my arms tightly against my chest.

Lilian stays quiet. I think she's waiting for me to spill.

I lick my lips and slowly turn to her. Little by little, my troubles trickle out. The new hairdo, the boys, the gum.

When I'm finished, Lilian shakes her head. "Horrid lads. I reckon you were able to rectify the situation?"

"I cut it out."

"You cut the gum from your hair? All on your own? Let me see, child."

I'm not about to argue with Lillian. Besides, my ponytails have been so tight lately my scalp practically sighs in relief when I set my hair free.

"Turn around, please."

I do.

"Indeed, you did cut it by yourself. With a hacksaw so it seems."

I spin back around, my eyes stinging.

"Never mind, never mind. You are not to blame. Does your father know about this misfortunate event?"

I shake my head.

She offers me a cookie, the good kind dipped in chocolate. "I'll sort this," she says. "Not to worry."

When we've finished our tea, Lilian escorts me to my apartment. She raps on my door, which feels weird because I live there, but I wait with her anyway. Dad answers and looks surprised to see us.

"Good afternoon, Calvin, how lovely to see you." They chat about the rain for a minute and then Lilian says, "With so much on your plate with work and settling in I'd be remiss if I didn't provide you with this." She produces a business card. "A hair salon, nearby on the high street. Very reputable."

Dad takes the card and runs his hand through his shaggy hair. "Oh. Yes. I suppose I am overdue."

Lilian gives him a tight smile. "Hm. Perhaps. Although this salon might better suit Addie."

Dad looks at me, then back at Lilian.

Lilian points to the card. "If you call that number and request Natalia, she'll see to Addie's needs."

"Thanks, Lilian," Dad says.

"They do book up quickly so best not to delay."

"Okay."

Lilian doesn't move. She sniffs and looks at Dad in expectation. "Natalia," she repeats. "That's who you want to book for Addie."

Dad stands there, looking confused, until something like embarrassment washes over him. "I see. Right." He pulls his phone from his pocket and taps in the number from the card. He chats to someone. Speaks my name. Hangs up. "Eleven o'clock, Saturday."

"Splendid," Lilian says. "I'll leave you to your afternoon. Lovely to see you both." She clips down the stairs and closes herself in her apartment.

The following Saturday, Dad and I stroll to the hair salon. "You know if you wanted a haircut you could have asked me," he says.

"You're always busy."

"I'm sorry," he sighs. "I'm not good at keeping up with haircuts and grocery orders and those types of things."

"It's okay. It's just that… well, my hair really, really needs a cut."

He looks at me. "Your hair doesn't seem *that* long."

He's going to find out soon enough. I take a big breath, undo my ponytail, and turn around so he can behold the horror.

"Oh," he says.

I confess the whole story. Except for the part when I couldn't stop crying afterward in my room. When I'm done talking, Dad kisses the top of my head.

We find Lillian's salon. The door jangles as we enter a room with soft grey and white striped walls, pink lampshades, and glistening mirrors. Nothing like the ugly brown *Cut-n-Go* Dad would take me to back home.

The lady at the counter smiles at Dad. "Can I help you?"

I step forward. I tell her I'm Addie Brown and I have an appointment at eleven o'clock with Natalia. She tells Dad he has a competent daughter. I'm not sure what *competent* means but I promise myself to look it up later. Then another woman with giant hoop earrings and a jumble of brown curls piled high on her head approaches. "I am Natalia. Come."

She leads me to a swivel chair. She sits me down, runs her fingers through my hair and says, "What I do for you my young lady?"

I tell the story one more time. Boys. Gum. Scissors. She takes her time examining my horror and then stammers in her choppy English, "I fix your... Oh, how do you say... Your..." she trails off as she fingers the jagged patch and searches for words.

"Mistake?" I offer.

"Yes. *Mistake*. I fix. You happy. Okay?"

We move to a glistening sink where she washes my hair and massages my scalp with her long, manicured fingernails, sending tingles up my spine. Then she wraps my hair in a fluffy towel and ushers me back to the swivel chair and asks what kind of haircut I want.

"One that makes my hair behave."

She grins and starts combing through. "Your hair wavy. I make work."

I'm curious about her accent and when I can't hold back any longer I ask, "Where are you from?"

"Bulgaria."

Another country to track down on a map. "What's Bulgaria like?"

She smiles. "Beautiful. My country... mountains, many trees." She stops clipping and gestures with her hands. "Tall trees. Cold. Snow in winter."

"Mine too! We have lots of tall trees and get tons of snow in my state."

While Natalia snips, she tells me about the big forest by her house in Bulgaria. I tell her about the sledding hill by mine.

"I think... you miss home?" Her thin eyebrows rise like two little hills.

In my mind I see Lauren, telling me she's not coming to London. That old awful lump creeps up my throat. I swallow hard. "Sometimes, I guess."

"Me too."

Natalia's fingers are fast but gentle. When she's finished cutting, she picks up a bottle and starts spritzing. I know that smell!

"*Citrus Curls*!"

"Is good. Will work for you."

This place is a dream come true factory. When she's all done, she spins my chair so I'm facing the mirror and I can't believe my eyes. I lean forward and touch my wonderfully curly tresses. Better than when Jasmine styled it! Natalia shows me the back. No traces that horrible Peter's disgusting gum ever lived in my hair. I hop down from the chair and thank her.

Dad gets up to pay. Natalia holds out a brand-new bottle of *Citrus Curls*. "You buy? For pretty daughter?"

I yank on his arm. "Please Dad, *please*?"

Dad agrees, pays, and once we step out of the best salon in London, suggests pizza at Aldo's for lunch. I hug him right there on the busy sidewalk.

There are two things I have to do before bed tonight:

1) Look up the word competent.

2) Thank Lilian.

That afternoon, for a split second, I want to call Lauren. I want to show her my hair. But then I remember her betrayal. I can't call her. If not her, then who? Parisa's parents don't let her FaceTime, Ellie and I have never talked outside of school before, and Victoria would only find something wrong and nit-pick it to death.

It's Lauren I want to talk to.

Doesn't our secret bracelet mean anything to her? So much for best friends forever.

I seize my planner. Flip to the last week of October. Stare at the words *Lauren in London* flocked with my hopeful hearts and flowers. I grab the corner of the page, rip it out, and tear the paper into a million pieces. And then, even though I know it's wrong, I push open my window and toss the scraps of a broken promise into the darkness below.

11

If Lauren feels guilty, I wouldn't know. She doesn't call or message or anything. It's been nearly two weeks. We've never gone this long without speaking to each other but I'm not about to make the first move.

"You haven't talked to Lauren in a while," Dad realizes one Saturday. "Do you want to call her tonight?"

I roll my eyes.

"What?"

"Nothing."

"Weren't she and her mom thinking of visiting London sometime?"

"Not anymore."

He looks at me for a moment. "Oh. That's too bad." Then he goes back to assembling his sandwich.

I shuffle to my room, close the door, and burst into tears. I can't help it.

Since I don't have a best friend to talk to, I suppose I might as well work on my essay for English. Write about a memory, Miss said. I sit at my desk and scribble out possible topics. The problem isn't thinking of something to write about, the problem is thinking of something to write about that won't embarrass the life out of you when you share it in front of the whole class. But that's part of the assignment Miss told us. We'll be marked on our presentation. Ugh.

I scribble out a list of ideas:

The time Lauren and I wrote a play and put on a show for the neighbors? No, too babyish.

The time I won the class spelling bee? No, too boring.

The time the cops showed up and told us Mom was in a car accident? No. Not that. Never ever.

I've got nothing to share.

On Monday at lunch I ask the gang what they've decided to write about.

"I'm writing about our ski chalet nestled in the spectacular Swiss Alps," Victoria declares.

"That doesn't sound like a memory," I say. "That sounds like a tourist advert."

"It *is* a memory. I've been there loads of times so I have loads of memories! I've already thought of a descriptive simile. *The snow covered the mountains like icing on a cake.*"

Rats, that's good. I was hoping it would be terrible since not only do I not own a ski chalet, I don't even have an essay topic. I noisily huff out my breath. "Well, I have no idea what to write about."

Victoria opens some chips – no, *crisps*. "You could write about the time you got gum stuck in your hair."

Parisa gives her a look. "That just happened."

"Still, it's a memory."

Ellie leans forward. "I'm writing about the time my brother cut his finger and bled all over the new sofa and my dad told him off for being reckless and the neighbour heard all the yelling and rang for an ambulance."

"Ellie," Victoria says, "do you really think your parents want you to share all of that?"

"Doubt it, but it's hilarious isn't it!"

Next day at Lilian's, I still haven't nailed down a topic. We're in the kitchen and Lilian is assembling morsels of food on a fancy looking three-tiered tower. "We have to share our essay in front the whole class," I tell her, eyeing a piece of chocolate cake with pink frosting. "And the class is full of dumb boys like Peter."

"I see. The assignment requires discretion."

Lilian carries her masterpiece to where I'm sitting at the table. Before my brain can stop my hand, I reach for the chocolate cake on the tippy top. Lilian gently tugs the food tower away. "Patience."

I clasp my hands together in my lap.

She sets the yellow teapot on the table and sits down. "Right then. The proper way to indulge in afternoon tea is to start at the bottom and work your way to the top."

Why not dive right into the good stuff, I want to suggest. The ground floor doesn't look half as exciting as the top floor. Lilian nudges the cake stand toward me.

I take a tiny rectangular sandwich and finish the morsel in two bites. "Can I have another one?"

"You certainly may. These are called finger sandwiches. The one you're eating is cucumber and dill. When must you submit your assignment?"

"Next week."

"Tell me, when did you arrive in London?"

"July. It was boiling hot when we flew out of Chicago and cold and rainy when we landed in London."

"What a transition that must have been. I expect it took some time to get used to all sorts of things, including living in your flat."

She's right. At first, moving into our apartment felt like living in a stranger's house with a stranger's furniture. Dad let me pick out a new bed with new sheets and a new quilt. Everything. But it wasn't until I rustled out my tattered turquoise blanket and furry pink pillows from a suitcase that I felt like the space was mine and I could breathe again. New things are great, but it's the old things that help you sleep at night and get you through the day.

Lilian takes a sip of tea. "Well, you're a clever girl. You'll think of something to write."

We've reached the middle level. We each take a scone, split them in half, spread on jam, then plop on clotted cream.

"Not nearly enough cream, Addie." Lilian piles more cream on my scone so that when I take a bite, cream gloriously fills the roof of my mouth.

Lilian hands me a napkin and asks how Dad is doing and if he likes working at the university. I can't really answer because I've never thought to ask.

We finish our scones. We've reached the top. The penthouse. The best of the best. Cake. Macrons. Sugar! Lillian smirks, deliberately making me wait. Finally, she gives me the go signal with the tip of her head. I swipe the chocolate morsel I've been dying to devour and finish the luscious thing in one bite.

"I'm as stuffed as a Thanksgiving turkey," I announce minutes later, leaning back in my chair.

Lilian strides to the kitchen. "When is Thanksgiving?" she asks as she pops a half of a cucumber, fresh dill, and cream cheese into a bag.

I stare at her. How can she not know? And then a horrible thought hits me. "You don't celebrate Thanksgiving?"

"Oh no. Not here." She hands me the bag. "Here are all the ingredients to make finger sandwiches. Perhaps you could make some for you and your father. Oh, and these." She adds two scones to the loot. "Mind you share."

The next morning, as Dad and I gobble up the scones, I announce that I'll be making supper that night. "Oh and guess what? They don't celebrate Thanksgiving here!"

Dad laughs. "No, of course not."

"Well, *we* have to."

Dad frowns. "I've never cooked a whole turkey before. Maybe we can simplify Thanksgiving. Roast a chicken. Bake some sweet potatoes. That kind of thing."

"No, we need to have a *real* Thanksgiving. Turkey and stuffing and cranberry sauce and pumpkin pie..."

"That's a lot of food for the two of us."

"We could invite Parisa. We could invite her whole family over!"

"I don't know, Addie. I'll have work that day and you'll have school. Thanksgiving is just an ordinary Thursday here in London."

How can such a wonderful holiday be a boring old Thursday? What a crime! How can you even *think* about celebrating Christmas without first celebrating Thanksgiving? Sweet potatoes with marshmallows and pumpkin pie piled high with whipped cream. Watching the Macy's Day Parade on TV in the morning and football – the American kind – in the afternoon. Playing games with your cousins and eating leftovers late at night and shopping with your Aunt the day after.

But nobody does that here. Thanksgiving doesn't belong in London and neither do I.

After school, I rush straight home. I turn the lock and push on the door, but it won't budge. It's caught on something. I give the door another shove and notice my hoodie poking through the crack. It must have tumbled out of the basket by the door that's supposed to keep us organized but only keeps toppling over. I manage to squeeze myself in. Scarves and gloves and jackets lay in heaps at my feet. I grab everything, shove it all back into the basket, and scowl at the disarray around me.

What happened to our apartment? When did it get so messy? When did Dad and I become slobs?

Ordinarily I wouldn't care. But tonight, I'm preparing dinner, for Dad and me, for the first time, and I want everything to be just right. I take off my school blazer, roll up my sleeves, and get to work.

I scramble around the living room collecting crumpled socks, stray candy wrappers, and coffee-stained cups and carry it all to the kitchen which... *Yikes!* Makes the living room look like a showroom. Thumbprints of jam stain the cupboard. Scone crumbs trail the counters. Dirty dishes stack up everywhere in leaning towers of disgustingness, and nobody put the orange juice away.

Where do I start? Where does it end? Where is Mary Poppins when you need her to swoop in, snap her fingers, sing a song, and fix your life? Maybe I could convince Lilian to convince Dad to hire a housecleaner. But that's not going to happen tonight. I guess it's up to me to put on my best Mary Poppins and whistle while I work.

Once the kitchen is reasonably tamed, I turn to the table buried in junk mail and school papers. I find a Tesco bag, swipe everything inside, and shove it into a cupboard. We don't have a tablecloth, Dad hasn't bothered to buy one, but I find a white sheet folded in the bathroom. I snap it open, drape it over the table, and top it with a stubby red candle I snagged from the back of the junk drawer. Better!

Now for the food.

I'm down to one last box of macaroni and cheese and Dad and I are going to savor it tonight. While I wait for the pot of water to boil, I spread cream cheese on bread, sprinkle with dill, top with cucumber circles, and cover with a second slice of bread. Then I cut the sandwich into dainty fingers. Just like Lilian's. We have salami and cheese in the fridge, so I make finger sandwiches out of that as well.

Thinking like a grown up, I hunt for a vegetable. Nothing but the same old bag of frozen peas. At least they add color. I dump some into a bowl, zap them in the microwave, then poke around in the fridge until I find fresh cherries.

Done! Macaroni and cheese, two types of finger sandwiches, buttered peas, and fresh cherries. The meal seems complete, the table looks pretty, and the apartment no longer looks like a war zone.

I'm pouring two glasses of sparkling water when Dad gets home. He takes in the room, stops in his tracks, and whistles. "Would you look at this!"

He sheds his workbag and suitcoat, then drops into a chair. I hand him a glass of water and sit down across from him. He raises his glass to me. "You've outdone yourself, Addie girl."

Feeling proud, I offer Dad the mac-n-cheese first. He scoops himself a portion and his phone trills. He glances at whatever message came through, then seizes his phone. "Oh no."

"What?"

"No, no, no. This is bad."

"What's bad?"

He hasn't looked up yet. "I forgot something. Something important."

"What did you forget?"

He stands and runs his fingers through his disheveled hair that really does need a cut. He looks at me in panic. "I'm supposed to take someone to dinner."

12

"What do you mean you're supposed to take someone to dinner?" I ask.

Dad's pacing now. "A while ago my boss arranged for me and a colleague to have dinner together."

"Now?"

"Yes, now. Right now, in fact."

"You're having dinner with your boss?"

"No, not my boss. With a lady called Elaina."

I drop my fork. "You have a *date*?"

"No, not a date. She's a colleague. From America, actually, visiting the university. My boss probably thought that since we're both Americans..."

"That you should take her on a *date*?"

"It's not a date!" Dad goes back to texting.

I huff. Dad's super lucky that he has such an understanding daughter who is big enough to adjust her plans. "Okay, fine," I say graciously. "Elaina can have dinner with us."

Dad doesn't look up from his phone. "That's kind of you, Addie, but I think she's expecting a little more than snack food."

Snack food? Did he just call my dinner *snack food*? After everything I've done? The whirlwind cleaning, the white tablecloth, the cooked peas, the carefully constructed sandwiches, it's not good enough for him and plan-wrecking, not-a-date date *Elaina*?

"Look, I'm really sorry Addie but I've got no choice. This is my job. I'll call Lillian…"

"I don't want Lilian." I didn't sacrifice my last box of mac-n-cheese for Lilian. I didn't run around the house like a girl on fire for Lilian.

"Maybe you could go to her place…"

"No. I'm fine."

He glances my way. "Are you sure? I'll stay close by. I'm telling Elaina to meet me at Aldo's, just down on the high street."

Has he lost his mind? Aldo's is *our* place. He shrugs into his suitcoat and smooths out his hair. "I'll be back before you know it. An hour and a half tops," he promises before dashing out the door.

I stare at the table, at all that I've slaved over. Dad's right. I've prepared snack food. Unevenly cut sandwiches. Shriveled peas. I take a nibble of the mac-n-cheese straight from the serving spoon. What should be warm and gooey tastes like paste. So much for savoring my last box. So much can change in the time it takes to snap your fingers.

I sit there for what feels like forever. Then suddenly I hurl the spoon across the room. It splats against the kitchen floor. Perfect. Now on top of everything else, I have a cheesy, orange mess to clean up.

Or maybe not. If Dad can just up and leave, why can't I?

I get up from the table, grab my hoodie, and set out. Where I'm going, I haven't a clue, but I'm heading somewhere. Anywhere but here.

The sun has long set in the November sky, but the high street shimmers with lights. I tip up my hood and set my sights on Aldo's red and white awning. As I approach the restaurant I slow my pace, trying to make out the faces of the people inside. Steps away from the front window, I stoop down and tie my shoe.

Dad's back is to me where he and a woman sit at a table by the window. *Our* table. Dad's and mine. Where Dad and I sat at our first visit to Aldo's, back before Dad let me ride the Tube by myself. I can't see Dad so he can't see me, but I can clearly see the woman. Elaina. She has short, streaky blonde hair and a dumb toothy smile. She's holding a goblet and listening to Dad. Suddenly, she tips her head back and laughs. She sets down her drink like she's afraid she might spill it and runs her fingers through her hair.

Who is this Elaina? Dad's not that funny.

Dad leans back in his chair, gesturing with his hands. Now it's Elaina turn to talk and Dad's turn to laugh. I've seen enough.

Not on a date? Yeah, right. And Mary Poppins cleaned my apartment.

I straighten up. Stick my hands in my pockets and feel the promise of my travel card. My ticket to anywhere. I adjust my hood and cross the street.

What if Dad spots me? Would he be surprised to see me waking alone on the high street? Would he leave Elaina and run after me? I make it to the station without any interruption. Either Dad didn't notice or didn't care.

I tap in, go through the barriers, and board the train just like I do for school. But when I get to Earl's Court, I don't change trains. I stay put. Today I'm not headed to school. Today I'm headed to the heart of the city. Zone one, here I come. Deep down I feel a spark of guilt, but my anger stamps it out and drives me forward, goading me on to break Dad's One Big Rule. Not break it a little bit, but smash it into smithereens.

He's going to be shocked! He's going to be furious! This big, bad thing I'm doing feels wild and satisfying, like bashing a piñata.

On I fly. When the train pulls into Westminster Station, I decide I've reached my stop. I step off as the people on the platform, weary from work, wait to step on. I'm running to the city and they can't wait to escape it and run home. Not me. Nothing at home for me but empty rooms and snack food. I follow the Way Out signs and dash up the steps that lead outside. But as I near the top I slow my pace. Right there smack in front of me, almost above me, looms a huge bronze pillar. I look up, and up.

There he is. Big Ben. Towering over me as stern as a school principal and majestic as a king. London's enormous, beautiful clock, the clock that Peter Pan and Wendy soar past on their way to Neverland. The clock Dad and I saw on our very first day in London. But not this close. Not shooting straight into the evening sky making me feel as small as a bird.

Small I may be but this bird flew all the way to Big Ben on her own.

Just then a little tune rings out from the tower and when the jingle ends, Big Ben sounds his chime, low and deep: *Dong! Dong! Dong! Dong! Dong! Dong! Dong!*

I feel like, somehow, he's urging me to turn around and go home. Could be, but who listens to clocks?

I cross the street with a flood of people flowing toward Parliament Square. I pause to greet the statue of Winston Churchill and say hello to the statue of Ghandi then carry on, block after block, until I find myself in Trafalgar Square with the great stone lions. On I go. Past the fountain and the National Portrait Gallery, down one street and then another, where businesspeople cluster beside brightly lit bars and couples enjoy cones of gelato. Too bad I didn't grab a fistful of coins from the jar in the kitchen on my way out.

I stride under Chinatown's dangling red lanterns and meander down streets growing narrower and louder. Westminster Station seems far away now.

These alley-like streets feel different – dark – and my hoodie gives little protection against the cold night air.

Better keep walking. Keep acting like everything's fine.

Clubs and tattoo parlors merge together along the snaky streets. The whole area feels like a party gone wrong. A party that shouldn't include me, a kid in a hoodie. A kid who should be home eating a bowl of ice cream and going to bed. I don't belong anywhere near here.

A group of women with tiny skirts cackle loudly as I pass.

A man slams a car door and spews swear words into his phone.

A drunk man asks me if I have any spare change.

I pick up my pace, heart galloping, legs wobbling. I want to go home. I feel in my pocket for my mobile. It's only a stupid old dumbphone but at least I can call Dad. It's not there. I've left it in my backpack.

Beginning to panic I spin around and search the night sky for the glow of Big Ben but I've strayed too far. Taken too many twists and turns. What if I end up like the homeless people on their dingy makeshift beds? Who will come and find me?

Head down. Keep moving. Keep pretending like I know what I'm doing and where I'm going. Carry on, carry on.

The blare of a siren startles me. I look up. Flashes of light and color from a giant video billboard shine up ahead. I know where I am. I've been here before. Crazy, feverish Piccadilly Circus.

I shuffle across the street to the fountain, the centerpiece for the wild party happening around it. Dancing, laughing, eating, drinking, but I don't slow down. I fix my eyes on the red circle with the blue bar and duck into the Underground as fast as I can.

Inside, the station is just as chaotic as the outside. I circle the station, bewildered, until I find a huge map. I stop. Stare at the colorful patterned lines snaking across the poster. I've seen these maps a million times before, but I've never actually bothered to read one.

It's as if someone has tossed a handful of colored yarn into the air and built a city around however the strands happened to land. *Think, Addie.* How do I make sense of this? What do I know?

I know that each circle designates a station and each line represents a track, but which dot is mine? Where is Piccadilly Circus and where is home and how do I go from where I am to where I am supposed to be?

Heart racing, hands shaking, I gape at the huge, indecipherable map. It's too much. All of it. This map, this city, this loneliness, this fear… I can't get around it. The lines on the map blur as tears fill my eyes.

"Need any help?" A voice says from behind me. A woman's voice. Gentle and kind.

Oh, how I want it to be her.

More than anything I want to turn around and see my mom. It's crazy. I know how death works. She's been gone for three years. She's not coming back. But if longing with all of your heart and wishing with all of your might let you bring back the dead, she would be here. Mom would scoop me up, take me home, and everything would be alright.

I turn around.

It's not her. Of course, it's not.

I stand frozen to the spot, spellbound by the lady in the green hat. Hair neatly tucked under her hat, jacket rustling in the breeze of the station, deep brown eyes penetrating mine as if she knows all of my secrets. Finally, this close, I can reach out and touch her. How I want to feel the warmth of her hand on mine and know for certain that she's real – flesh and bone, hopes and fears – just like me. But my body won't move.

"Let me help you," she says.

I can't do anything but meet her gaze. How does she always seem to be in the right place at the right time?

My mind is whirring but I can't speak.

"Let me help you," she says again.

Help? How can she help? Can she change the past? Can she bring Mom back? Can she put me on a train that travels back in time, to before Mom's car was hit by a truck on an icy road?

"I want my mom," I blurt out angrily.

The lady in the green hat looks at me calmly – almost like she didn't hear me. She doesn't shush me. She only nods, her eyes steady, like she's waiting for me to go on.

"She's not here and she should be here, and I want her back."

"Of course you do."

Why is she not surprised? It's like she already knows what I'm going to say before I say it.

"Everyone else has a mom. Why can't I? It's not fair."

"No, it's not."

The two of us stand face to face, like we're encased in a bubble, the flurry of the world spinning around us. I'm vaguely aware of other people, walking by, looking at me.

Never before have I spoken these words out loud. Not that I can remember anyway. Something has been unleashed in me and I go on.

"And… I don't like it here. In London. I miss home. Why did my dad move us here? I wish we were back home."

The lady in the green hat doesn't sing the praises of living in London or scold me for questioning Dad. She doesn't give me that grown up look like she knows everything, and I know nothing. She simply waits, listening, as if she has all the time in the world. As if what I'm saying matters. The words that have been choking me for so long have been released and I feel a little stronger. Like I can focus on what needs to be done.

I wipe my eyes. Face the map. So many lines. So many dots. So many possibilities of routes to travel and places to live. The lady in the green hat studies the lines and circles with me.

"Where do you belong?" she asks.

If there was a train that could transport me home to Wisconsin, would I take it? *Is* Wisconsin still home? Or would I hop on the next train back to Putney, back to our apartment and my fuzzy pink pillows and Lilian downstairs. Which home would I choose? Where *do* I belong?

"I don't know," I finally admit.

"Perhaps you don't know *where* you belong," she says, placing the tip of her finger on the Piccadilly Circus dot, "but surely you know to *whom* you belong." Her long finger glides along the blue line until it reaches Earl's Court. There it is! I can take it from here.

I press my own finger on Earl's Court and slide it along the green line until it hits East Putney.

Home.

The weight of my crime crashes into me. What have I done? I've broken Dad's One Big Rule. I've ignored what he said and did what I wanted and got all mixed up and now all I want to do is get back to him.

Is he home? Is he waiting for me?

I picture Dad leaving Aldo's, heading back to our apartment, and opening the front door. I see him standing in the kitchen, confused by the table full of food. He calls my name. No one answers. He strides to my room. I'm not there. He runs to his room. It's empty. He races to the living room and calls for me again and again, but no one answers because I've run off.

"Dad!" I whisper. I turn to the lady in the green hat. "I need to go home. I need to get home to Dad."

She nods. "Come with me."

We sail down the escalators and board a train. At Earl's Court we take another train that drops us at East Putney. I tap out, rush past the purple flower hut, and am halfway down the street when I stop. I forgot to thank her. I spin around, but the lady in the green hat is nowhere to be seen.

No matter.

Right now, all that matters is Dad.

13

Dad's a block up ahead, jogging on the sidewalk, looking every which way. I've never seen that look of terror on his face before.

I break into a run. "Dad!"

He sees me and his face crumples. I jump into his open arms.

"I'm sorry Dad. I'm so sorry!" He pulls me in and holds me tight and then tighter.

"Addie, are you okay?"

I tell him I'm fine and it's the truth. I'm back, he's here, and everything's going to be alright.

When we untangle from each other he says, "What were you thinking? What in the world made you run off?"

"You left. I made dinner but then you went off on a date."

Dad closes his eyes for a second. "That was rotten of me. I should have cancelled. But it wasn't a date, it was a work dinner."

"It sure looked like a date."

He lets out his breath. "What do I know? Maybe it was a date. But Addie, I *am* allowed to meet up with other grown-ups. I *can* have dinner with a woman. I could even have a date if I wanted to. That's no reason for you to disobey and run away."

"I know. I'm sorry." I can feel the overwhelming urge to cry rising through my body but I push it back down as far as I can.

He studies me for a moment, his hands still clutching my shoulders, as if he wants to make sure it's really me and I'm really here. Then we turn and start walking slowly down the high street. There's so much I could tell him about what I heard and saw tonight. Big Ben and Trafalgar Square, crazy Piccadilly Circus and the encounter with the lady in the green hat. But right now, all I want to do is snuggle underneath the protection of his arm and go home.

We stroll past businesspeople coming home late from work. We pass the Vietnamese restaurant and the bright smell of ginger fills my nose. "Dad? Why did we move here? Was it to get away from Mom?"

He stops. "What?"

"I heard you tell Aunt Becky that we moved to London to get away from Mom."

"No, honey. Your mom will always be a part of us." We continue on down the sidewalk. "In a way, maybe I moved to London to get closer to her."

Now it's my turn to stop and stare.

And then he tells me about the time he and Mom visited London, when they were first married, before I was born. He tells me how they took a river cruise down the Thames and cycled through Hyde Park. "Your mother loved London," he says, "especially the Tube. She said zipping around the city made her feel wild and free, like she was part of a story with limitless possibilities. Sometimes we'd jump on a train, not knowing exactly where we were going, and hop off to find ourselves in a whole new world. The Docklands. Brick Lane. Chinatown. I'll have to take you there someday."

I duck my head and smile. I picture my mom sailing along on the Underground, just like me. We've ridden the same Tube. Sat in the same seats maybe, stood on the same platforms. She knew about the crazy hidden world below our feet.

I take a big breath and let it out. "I miss her. I wish she were here."

Dad doesn't crumble. He doesn't fall to pieces at my confession. "I do too."

I don't want him to stop talking about her, I want him to go on and on all night. "Tell me something else about Mom."

We stroll in silence while Dad thinks. "Your mom," he finally says, "was notorious for leaving half-eaten apples around the house."

"What?"

"She did it all the time. She'd start munching on one, set it down, and move on to something else and forget all about it. I'd find half-eaten apples all over the place. On the counter, in the bathroom, in the bed…"

I giggle. "You would not!"

"Okay maybe not in the bed, but I'd find them everywhere and I'd always feel obliged to finish them. That was your mom. Enthusiastically bouncing from one thing to the next."

I imagine her, flowing brown hair trailing behind, snacking on an apple until *bing!* A light bulb appears above her head! And off she flits leaving her apple behind.

He looks at me. "I see that same zest for life in you."

His words warm me like a mug of tea warms your hands.

We pass the homeless man and his sad looking dog. Dad drops a few coins into the cup. I shiver and Dad takes off his suitcoat and drapes it around me, the sleeves swinging down to my thighs. "Dad? Do you ever want to get married again?"

He grins. "Who would want to marry a boring old professor like me?"

"Mom did."

He laughs. "I don't know, Addie. Maybe someday."

I sigh. "I guess you're not *that* old."

He shoves me lightly. "Thanks. Some people would say forty is still quite young."

We turn down the passageway that leads to our building and I suddenly remember the mess of food I left on the table. "Well, if you ever do go on a date again, can you do it on a night I haven't made mac-n-cheese?"

"Never again." He squeezes my shoulder. "You know you're my everything, right?"

Saturday morning. Time to dance. I've just strapped on my tap shoes and am clicking my way to the kitchen floor when Dad tells me to put on work clothes. "Why?" I demand.

"Because Lilian mentioned she had sorting and cleaning to do and you're going to help her. That's your punishment."

Ugh! Not off the hook. I should have known a consequence for breaking Dad's One Big Rule was coming even though I've promised a million times that I've learned my lesson and will never run away to the city again. Even so, Dad *still* makes me turn in my travel card when I get home from school every day.

"Did you tell Lilian about what happened?" I moan.

"I need to turn to somebody for parenting advice!"

I slump to my room, tug on a pair of tattered jeans and an old camp t-shirt that's getting too small and, minutes later, knock on Lilian's door, braced for a scolding.

"Ah, my apprentice for the day," Lilian says when she opens the door. "Come through, Addie, come through." And wonder of wonders, that's all she says. Maybe she really was a girl once and knows what it's like to mess up, feel stupid, and wish everyone around you would not say a word about it.

I follow her to the kitchen which is drowning in cardboard boxes and clear containers.

"Lilian are you moving?" I exclaim, suddenly realizing she can't. I'd miss her too much, tea and all.

"Goodness no."

"Well then are you throwing a party and having people over?"

"I'm throwing things *out* and redistributing the excess."

Earl Grey, sitting among the jumble, gazes up at me in apprehension. I slowly crouch down and slide my finger along the floor until it's touching one of his paws. He doesn't flinch! I reach to pet under his chin, but he scrambles away. It's progress.

"Everything must be cleaned and sorted," Lilian instructs. "My son will take some of these things and most of the dishes will go to a charity that helps others start over."

"Start over what?"

"With life, I suppose. My friend assists people who've escaped difficult situations. She mentioned she was desperate for kitchen items and I said my kitchen was desperate for a proper cleanout." She taps a box with her finger. "You can start sorting through this one."

I peel off the strip of packing tape and remove mugs, bowls, and salt and pepper shakers, until my fingers come across something large and solid. I lift out the bundle, unwrap the tissue paper, and uncover a turquoise serving platter. "How pretty!"

Lilian turns to me. "It is, isn't it? Yet another peacock gift from Nigel."

I take a better look. She's right. I didn't notice at first, but the glossy ceramic platter is covered in dark blue "eyes", like the design of a peacock's tail. "Nigel liked giving you peacock presents?"

"Quite. Starting with this," she says, fingering the tiny bird pendent resting on her chest. "It became rather like a sport for him."

I glance around the room and spy a small, framed peacock print on the wall, a peacock dishtowel hanging on a hook, and the corner of a peacock print pillow peeking out from the couch. "Why? Just because you like them?"

Lilian smirks. "Would you believe he claimed I reminded him of one? Such nonsense. Besides, everyone knows it's the *male* peacock who struts and flaunts. *He's* the show-off."

"Good thing, too."

Lilian looks at me quizzically from where she's standing at the sink.

"Peacocks are meant to show-off. If they never did, we'd never get to enjoy their beautiful tails. Why keep such a magnificent thing all tucked away? If you have something good to share, I say share it."

I hand Lilian the platter. She studies me for a moment before submerging the bright peacock dish into the soapy water.

Later that evening, Dad hollers that Aunt Becky wants to talk to me. I zip to the table to find Aunt Becky's beaming face on Dad's computer screen.

"Hello gorgeous!" she says. "Have I got news. Guess who's coming to London for Thanksgiving?"

"Who?"

She drums her hands on her table. "None other than your favorite aunt!"

"For real? But that's like in two weeks!"

"Yes, and I cannot *wait* to see you!"

"That's so great! But wait, Aunt Becky. People here don't celebrate Thanksgiving."

She erupts with laughter. "Well, *we* are certainly going to celebrate it! Let me tell you!"

"Can you bring some things?"

"Name it."

I ask for the puffy mini marshmallows, the stuffing that comes in the red box, and candy corn.

"You got it," she says.

I whoop and holler and clap my hands. "Yes! A real Thanksgiving, with me and you and Dad..." I stop. That's only three people. It still isn't enough. "And maybe my friend Parisa?"

"Absolutely. Can't wait to meet her."

"And maybe... her whole family?"

"The more the merrier."

"And Lilian from downstairs?"

"Hang on, hang on," Dad says, shoving me over slightly so he can see Aunt Becky on the screen. "How big is this dinner party going to get?"

"Calvin. This is your older sister speaking. Addie can invite whomever she wants."

"Within reason."

"*Whomever she wants,*" Aunt Becky bellows.

"But I only have six chairs."

Aunt Becky dramatically throws back her head. "You're killing me, Cal. We'll find chairs. I'll *buy* chairs if need be. This is *Thanksgiving*, you old stick in the mud."

"Yeah, you old stick in the mud," I mimic. Dad gives me a sharp look. I press my lips together.

"Don't worry," Aunt Becky says. "Addie and I will handle everything. You won't have to lift a finger. Which means you don't get a say in any of it. Nothing. *Nada*."

"*Rien*," I say the word tumbling out in French.

"Okay, okay," Dad finally says. "I get it. I'm overruled. You two crazies handle Thanksgiving however you see fit."

I grab my planner. Turn past the page I tore out. For the next ten minutes, Aunt Becky and I dream and plan. By the time we hang up, I have lists and doodles galore.

On the fresh page beside it, I plant my palm smack in the middle. Starting at my wrist below my thumb, I trace my hand. Up and down, around each finger, until I reach the edge of my wrist below my pinky. I remove my hand, connect the gap at the bottom, add feet, eyes, a beak, and the most important bit, a dangling wattle.

It's what every American kid makes in November: a turkey hand. Even if they live in London. The pages fall back to the gap where the *Lauren in London* page used to be.

I still haven't talked to her. And I still really miss her. But I still haven't a clue what to do about it.

14

I wish Miss would put me out of my misery.

One by one she calls students to the front of the class to read their English essay. I'd rather get my presentation over and done with than sit here like a sweaty ball of nerves.

Parisa's up next. She describes her day at the beach where, "The water shined like glass."

Victoria's turn. She tells us her family's Swiss Chalet is "As pretty as a castle in the snow."

Peter's essay is short and boring. He claims that his favorite team winning the big match was "Like a brilliant victory."

"Thank you, Peter," Miss says when he's finished. "However, inserting the word *like* does not a simile make."

I snicker as Peter shuffles back to his desk and slumps in his chair.

"Addie Brown?"

Yikes!

"Your essay please?"

Right. I fumble with the paper. Take my place at the front. Take a breath and read:

The day I moved to London, my Aunt Becky drove Dad and me to the airport. She cried when we said goodbye. It was the last goodbye after hundreds of goodbyes. Getting on the plane felt like getting to the end of a long roller coaster line and wanting to turn around. You begin to wonder, maybe you're not ready for all the hills and dips. But when you're a kid you don't have a choice, so you get on and hold on tight to whatever you can.

I stop for a second and look at the class. Everyone is looking at me. Eyes fixed as if held in a trance. My hand is shaking. My heart is thumping. I feel like it's so loud the others must be able to hear it. I take the deepest breath I can, look back at my paper and stare hard at the words on the page.

After we landed in London, when Dad opened the front door to our new apartment, he said, "Welcome home". But it wasn't home. It wasn't anything like our house in America with the green shutters and the big back yard. Everything and everyone we knew was far away. That's the hard thing about moving to a new country. Parts of you end up left behind. It's like you've been divided into pieces, like a human jigsaw puzzle…

Someone laughs. Horrible Peter? I look to Miss. She nods. I clear my throat and start the sentence over.

It's like you've been divided into pieces, like a human jigsaw puzzle and pieces of you are scattered all over or missing. It's okay now. Our apartment sort of feels like a home, but my old house still feels like home, too. Both places are home because both places hold pieces of me.

I lay the paper on my teacher's desk as instructed and walk back to my seat.

"I'll say pieces are missing," Peter mutters.

When the bell rings Miss says, "Addie?" and motions me forward.

What have I done now? I check my neck for my tie. And I'm all buttoned up. Victoria gives me a warning look as she and everyone else stream out the door.

I approach Miss who's reading an essay at her desk. It's *my* essay. There's some cursive scrawled at the bottom and I only notice two small red marks in the body. Miss sets the paper down and looks up. "Well done on your essay, Addie."

I sigh in relief. "Thank you, Miss."

"You express your thoughts well and your comparisons were fresh and effective. Listening to your essay made me think of Poland."

"Is that your home?"

She nods. "It is. As is London. But you know all about that." She uncaps her pen and scribbles something at the bottom of the paper and then holds it out to me. "You may take this with you. Share it with your father."

I take the paper. Underneath her comments sits a big, beautiful *A*.

When I get home from school, I grab an apple from the fruit bowl and show Dad my essay. As I munch, he reads it slowly and quietly. When he's done, he looks up and smiles. He gets up, tousles my hair, and secures my essay smack dab in the middle of the fridge before heading down the hall.

I take a few more strategic bites of my apple. Then I set the half-eaten apple on the middle of the counter for Dad to find later.

Everything about Aunt Becky is big. Big hair, big teeth, big voice, big hugs.

A few days before Thanksgiving, when she spots Dad and me waving at the arrival gate at Heathrow, she abandons her big pink suitcase, lunges for me, and pulls me tight against her big chest. Her strong arms feel good. She releases me to hug Dad, but then seizes me again, crying like a baby and not trying to be quiet about it.

Oh yeah. Big emotions, too.

I've given up my bed for Aunt Becky. We'll share my bedroom and I'll sleep on the air mattress that plugs into the wall and inflates by itself. While Aunt Becky unzips her suitcase, I transfer my blankets and pillows to the airbed.

“So,” Aunt Becky says, lining up her toiletry items on the top of my desk. “Give me the scoop. The good, the bad, the ugly. How are things?”

I shrug. “Sometimes good, sometimes bad.”

“Let’s start with the bad. What don’t you like about living here?”

I plop down on the air mattress and clutch my pillow. “I still don’t like tea.”

Aunt Becky laughs. “Boy are you in the wrong country!”

“But I manage to get it down with Lilian.”

“Not a lover of tea. What else?”

I think for a moment. “I’m not crazy about my Math teacher or wearing a tie. And there are lots of rules here about how you should act and what you should say but nobody tells you the rules, you have to figure them out for yourself. And I miss my old room and my backyard.” I fiddle with the string on my hoodie. “And Lauren.”

“I’m sure she misses you, too.”

I pick up Aunt Becky’s eye shadow case and thumb open the lid to view the colors. “No she doesn’t. She didn’t come to visit me like she said she would.”

Aunt Becky sits down on the bed. “That hurts. A lot, I’m sure. But I have no doubt that Lauren misses you and still likes you. The two of you have been friends for a long time and now you each have to work out how to go about your days without each other. You can still be friends, but it’ll be different.”

“But I really wanted to show her London.”

"Of course you did. What would you have shown her?"

"How to ride the Tube and how to scramble up to the top of a bus without falling down the stairs and how to shop on the high street and run through the pigeons in the park."

Aunt Becky goes back to her suitcase. "Sounds like you kind of like it here."

She's right. I suppose. And I haven't even mentioned Parisa or Lilian or my English teacher, the West End, Tower Bridge, Chinatown, or Big Ben. London is pretty cool, when I stop to think about it. Out of all the cities Dad could have moved us to, I guess he picked a pretty good one.

"You look like you fit right in," Aunt Becky says.

"I do?"

"When we rode the Tube from the airport this morning, you knew exactly what to do and where to go. A true Londoner."

I sit up a bit taller. Maybe I could belong in this city. But can you belong in one place and still miss another?

"My guess," Aunt Becky says as she refolds a pair of trousers, "is that you feel stuck between the two, home and here. Or maybe it's home and *there*. Whichever it is, you can enjoy your new life *and* miss your old one." Aunt Becky sits down across from me and looks me in the eye.

That's Aunt Becky. She dives right in and then waits for you to join her in the deep end. But she's right. *Home* is no longer a fixed, sure place or a simple word to define.

I can't pin it down. Home is runny and complicated, like painting with watercolours.

"And you're allowed to miss your mom."

I look away and bite my lip. "I've tried really hard not to miss her," I venture after a while.

"Sweetie, why? You *should* miss your mom. You'll always miss your mom. I still do and I was only her sister-in-law."

I hug the pillow tighter. "But I don't want to be sad all the time."

"No, of course not. But we can't escape sadness. Grief pops up over and over again, sometimes when we least expect it."

Like the lady in the green hat.

"And when it does, best to face it. Pay it some attention."

"How?"

"When you're sad, feel sad. When you miss your mom, miss your mom. And then if in the next moment you find yourself laughing with your friends, laugh with your friends. Don't bottle things up and keep it all inside. Heaven knows your mother didn't!"

"She didn't?"

Aunt Becky laughs. "Not at all. Isabella wore her beautiful heart on her sleeve." Aunt Becky gives my ankle a gentle squeeze. "And you are her daughter."

She goes back to her suitcase, shaking out and folding clothes, lining up containers and cosmetics on my desk, and I'm content to watch her. Aunt Becky is here, in London, in my room, and right now there's no place I'd rather be.

15

Pumpkin pies? Baked and cooling.

Turkey roasting in the oven? To a crispy golden brown.

Table moved to the living room and set for eight? With a brand-new tablecloth Aunt Becky and I picked out at M&S and two chairs Dad bought at a charity shop. The place doesn't look anything like the sloppy sty it was a couple of weeks ago.

Someone knocks on the door and I run to open it. There stands Lilian holding a dish tented with aluminum foil.

"Happy Thanksgiving!" Aunt Becky bellows from behind me. She strides toward us wearing fuzzy slippers, her apron dotted with cross-eyed turkeys, and a great big grin.

Standing between these two opposites, I suddenly feel jittery. What if small, silver-haired Lilian who rarely laughs clicks her tongue in disapproval at tall, colorful Aunt Becky who is hardly ever quiet? What if crazy Aunt Becky bear hugs Lilian? What if my two worlds colliding only ends in chaos?

Aunt Becky thrusts out her hand. "You must be the Lilian from downstairs that I've heard so much about. Wonderful to meet you."

Lilian smiles and accepts the handshake. "And you must be Aunt Becky from America. The pleasure is entirely mine."

Aunt Becky takes the platter and links arms with Lilian, and the two of them chatter their way to the kitchen like they've known each other forever.

The doorbell buzzes. I hit the button to let Parisa and her family into the building. When I open our door, Jasmine hands me a bouquet of flowers before I lead them to the kitchen and introduce everybody to everybody else.

Our apartment has never felt so full. Parisa, Jasmine, and I finish setting the table while Aunt Becky, Lilian, and Parisa's mom bustle about in the kitchen. Dad and Parisa's dad hang in the living room where Dad tries to explain the rules of American football. I'm hunting for more serving spoons when Aunt Becky slides the sweet potatoes from the oven and sprinkles them with mini marshmallows.

"Marshmallows on sweet potatoes?" Lilian asks.

"You bet," Aunt Becky says. "It'll knock your socks off, Lilian. Just you wait."

Lilian looks amused. She peels back the foil covering the dish she brought and I gasp.

"The peacock platter! You kept it!"

"I'm not keeping it."

I look at the platter, confused.

"It's for you."

"Really?"

I thank her and promise to be careful with it but Lilian waves my words away with her hand. "Seemed fitting. One proud bird deserves another," she says with a nod toward the golden-brown turkey Dad's carving.

I set the platter of Lillian's Yorkshire puddings on the table and return to the kitchen to hear Parisa's mom tell Aunt Becky that the dish she brought is made from aubergine, tomatoes, and turmeric.

"Don't worry, aubergine is just eggplant," I assure Aunt Becky when Parisa's mom is out of earshot. "Taste it, even if it looks weird."

Aunt Becky chuckles. "I absolutely will."

Parisa and I carry dish after dish to the table. "What is this?" Parisa whispers, glancing at the one in her hands.

"Stuffing."

"*Stuffing?*"

"You'll love it." I promise.

"But... what *is* it?"

She's afraid of harmless, American stuffing! I regard the brown and yellow lumps speckled with green. I guess it does look kind of gross, if you're not used to it. "It's bits of bread with herbs. It's good. Taste and see."

Finally, when the turkey and cranberry sauce, stuffing and green bean casserole, marshmallow topped sweet potatoes and mashed potatoes and gravy, corn casserole and Jello salad, are nestled beside the English Yorkshire puddings and Iranian eggplant – neither of which I'm afraid to try – we sit down. All of us. Eight smiling faces around my table.

Aunt Becky prays. We echo *Amen!* and the food goes around the table. When Parisa's father asks what Thanksgiving is about, Dad explains how the English pilgrims sailed to America in 1620 on a ship called the Mayflower that landed in Plymouth Rock.

"Not only was it a grueling voyage," Dad says, "but half of the pilgrims died from sickness, starvation, and the cold harsh winter that first year."

"Why did the pilgrims leave England?" Parisa's mom wants to know.

"They wanted to worship God in greater freedom," Aunt Becky answers. "Without restriction. They left everything to start over in a foreign land."

Parisa's father nods. "This we understand,"

"And the Native Americans helped the pilgrims," I say, trying to hurry up the history lesson, "and then at harvest time they all came together for one big feast."

"Right," Dad says. "Even though they were missing home and grieving their losses, they set time aside to give thanks."

"I see," Parisa's dad says. "Thanksgiving is about coming together."

"And thanking God for his goodness," Aunt Becky adds.

"Even when times are difficult," Parisa's mother says softly.

Aunt Becky gives Parisa's mom one of her warmest smiles.

I scoop some sticky sweet potatoes into the cavity of my Yorkshire pudding and shove half of the doughy goodness into my mouth. "From now on," I announce, "we shall have Yorkshire puddings at every Thanksgiving!"

Dad frowns. "Addie, swallow before you speak."

But Lilian's eyes twinkle as she helps herself to more sweet potatoes.

After dinner, we play games. Then Dad shows a clip of the Macy's Thanksgiving Day Parade and Aunt Becky and I serve tea and coffee. Then I step away for a moment to message Lauren.

Gobble gobble. Happy Thanksgiving!! I include a turkey and pumpkin emoji.

It doesn't take long for Lauren to message back:

Happy Thanksgiving! I miss you.

Beside her message sit two purple hearts.

It's not much but it's something. Like reaching out and touching the tip of Earl Grey's paw. You have to start somewhere.

When Aunt Becky takes out the pumpkin pies from the fridge, I tell her that I can serve them on my own.

"Wonderful," she says and puts her feet up in the living room next to Jasmine.

I'm dividing one of the pies into triangles when Dad comes into the kitchen. "Need any help?"

"Nope. I've got this, Dad."

"I know you do, Addie girl. My amazing Addie who organizes Thanksgiving dinner and navigates the Tube and puts up with her Dad's glum moods and mediocre cooking..."

"Your burgers aren't bad."

"...and who's handled so many changes like a champ." He kisses my forehead. Then, would you believe it? He plunges his pinky right into the middle of my pumpkin pie, pulls it out and licks it clean.

"Dad!"

"Just testing to make sure it's done."

I shove him out of the kitchen, back to our guests, to our friends and family who are drinking tea and laughing and looking like they belong here.

They do belong here.

And so do I.

16

We're at Waterloo Station when I see her again. Dad, Aunt Becky, and I are out for a day of sight-seeing and we've just stopped to check our directions when I glimpse the familiar flash of green.

"Dad! Can I have some money to buy a drink?"

Dad, preoccupied with the map on his phone, hands me a few coins, and I rush off after the lady in the green hat. It's my chance to thank her. For showing up and listening. For getting me home when I was lost. For being her wonderful, mysterious self.

I sprint after her as she turns down a corridor, promising myself not to go any further than this. But we run into a platform, and she rushes to board the waiting train.

"Wait!" I call, reaching my hand toward her.

She doesn't hear and slips through the closing door. Then she turns around, spots me, and smiles from behind the window.

The lights in the carriage flicker. Light to dark, light to dark. But it's not only the train lights wavering, I realize.

It's *her*. The lady herself. The edges of her glimmer and glint, her body blips and blurs like a fuzzy picture on an old television screen. As the train begins to crawl away, I follow alongside of it, transfixed.

Poof! The lights in the train go out. Blackness. But only for a moment. *Blink!* Light returns but the lady does not. Just like that, she is gone, transported back to whatever secret world she's come from, like lightning flashing through the sky and vanishing just as suddenly. She was here a second ago. This time I'm sure of it.

This is no ordinary lady.

Spellbound, I watch the train disappear into the tunnel. Then I make my way back to my family.

"Did you get what you wanted?" Dad asks when he sees me.

It takes me a moment to realize he's talking about a drink. "No," I say my mind whirling. "But that's okay. Maybe another time."

What just happened? Whatever it is, it's wonderful. Crazy, but wonderful. I tuck away the scene to take out and explore later. Someday maybe I'll unravel the mystery of the lady in the green hat, but not today. Right now, I've got a city to see.

We've got fish and chips to munch and Tower Bridge to cross and shops to peruse and a hundred other things to do and taste and experience in this land I love and loathe, this fascinating and frustrating city that's now a part of me.

We exit the station and step outside. After so many drab grey days, the startling blue sky and stark white clouds that tower above us like heaps of cream make you think anything is possible. Dad, Aunt Becky, and I pause on the steps. We may be blocking foot traffic but that's okay. A view like this deserves your full attention, at least for a second.

"Hello London," I say.

Then the three of us link arms, clip down the steps, and join the rhythm of the city.

About the Author

Originally from the American Midwest, Rachel Allord lives in London where she serves with ReachGlobal and writes books and resources. She's married with two adult children and has a deep fascination with London's Underground. *The Girl on the Tube* is her third novel. Connect with her at rachelallord.com.